I0393154

Taking the Next Step

to living your

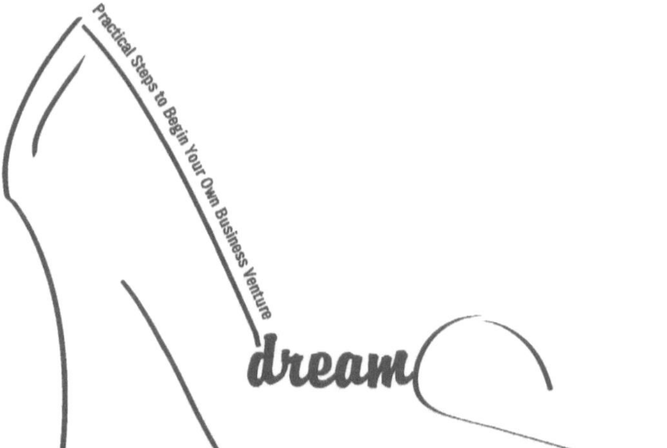
Practical Steps to Begin Your Own Business Venture
dream

Includes Thought Provoking Questions to Ponder After Each Chapter

Melissa Palmer

outskirtspress
DENVER, COLORADO

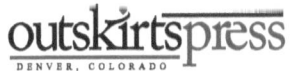

The opinions expressed in this manuscript are solely the opinions of the author and do not represent the opinions or thoughts of the publisher. The author has represented and warranted full ownership and/or legal right to publish all the materials in this book.

Taking The Next Step To Living Your Dreams
Practical Steps To Begin Your Own Business Venture
All Rights Reserved.
Copyright © 2014 Melissa Palmer
v2.0

Cover Photo © 2014 Melissa Palmer. All rights reserved - used with permission.

This book may not be reproduced, transmitted, or stored in whole or in part by any means, including graphic, electronic, or mechanical without the express written consent of the publisher except in the case of brief quotations embodied in critical articles and reviews.

Outskirts Press, Inc.
http://www.outskirtspress.com

ISBN: 978-1-4787-2612-8

Outskirts Press and the "OP" logo are trademarks belonging to Outskirts Press, Inc.

PRINTED IN THE UNITED STATES OF AMERICA

Table of Contents

CHAPTER 1 – YOU'RE FIRED! 1

CHAPTER 2 – FAITH VS. PATIENCE 16

CHAPTER 3 – ANGELA: A CASE STUDY OF FAITH 26

CHAPTER 4 – GETTING INTO THE GAME / BEING A
    PROVERBS 31 WOMAN 32

CHAPTER 5 –GOALS – THE WRITTEN WORD 45

CHAPTER 6 – LEAD GENERATION 52

CHAPTER 7 – PERSEVERING THROUGH THE PROCESS 59

CHAPTER 8 – LISA: A CASE STUDY IN PERSEVERANCE 67

CHAPTER 9 – 7 KEY COMPONENTS TO EFFECTIVE
    TIME MANAGEMENT 73

CHAPTER 10 – NEW BUSINESS DEVELOPMENT 80

CHAPTER 11 – SOCIAL MEDIA 85

CHAPTER 12 – MARKETING AND ADVERTISING 92

CHAPTER 13 – STACY: A CASE STUDY IN INDEPENDENCE 99

CHAPTER 14 - NETWORKING 104

CHAPTER 15 – REBECCA: A CASE STUDY FROM
    TRAGEDY TO TRIUMPH 111

CHAPTER 16 – INSPIRING OTHERS 115

CHAPTER 17 – MELODY: A CASE STUDY IN INSPIRATION 120

CHAPTER 18 -MEASURING SUCCESS 124

Introduction

My mission in writing this book is to encourage women, who have a dream of owning their own business, or to help and encourage those already in business who may need to get to the next level. For those who need help in taking the first steps of beginning their business, my hope is they will realize their gifts and talents as God created them, and use them to their full potential. My dream is women of all ages will be moved to take their next step of faith, whether that be starting a bakery, jewelry store or consulting business, or simply encouraging those who have gone before me to persevere to the next level to be the best business owner they can be!

Why Write This Book?

After starting my own business, I had multiple networking opportunities with other women. I sought them out, as a matter of fact, to gather as much information as possible to help my start up…things like marketing, advertising, social media and flat out simple encouragement. Some of them you will meet throughout this book. What I realized, is after meeting with these women, THEY came away inspired by me, just as much as I was encouraged by them. I could not keep this to myself! I realized there is such a powerful force when women get together, understand their value and share ideas.

One encounter was a woman whom I knew of from my same industry who ventured out on her own. I had researched her website and her background, and realized she was about my age. I was impressed. I called her and she accepted my offer for coffee. After about 2 hours of chatting about our backgrounds and hearing her amazing story of risk taking, we both came away inspired and refreshed.

Another encounter stemmed from that first coffee meeting and our sharing of contacts. She directed me to another woman who had started her own business almost ten years ago and it was going strong.

Again I felt intrigued and inspired to call her. During the course of that call, I realized I was doing most of the encouraging. Sharing about how to generate new leads and how to stay motivated in the midst of a slow economy was exactly what she needed to hear at that time.

After both conversations, these women were telling me how I had helped them gain a new zest for their businesses. They were encouraged to forge ahead; maybe when they were close to giving up on their dreams, all the while inspiring me. This was the catalyst to writing this book.

In Proverbs 31, (Prov 31:15-22 NASB) it says the ideal woman (or woman of worth) rises early and takes care of feeding her family. She also invests in land, plants crops and watches for the harvest. She works hard to make clothing for her children and herself...she dresses in fine linen and purple. The idea of the working woman is not a new concept; however, society has skewed it a bit. Women have unique gifts and talents that, simply put, men do not possess. My goal is to help empower women, not as society and women's liberation have done in a negative manner, but as God has designed us, beautiful, intelligent, successful and balanced. We, as women, need to remember that while we have specific roles, we want to be sure not to cross the lines of emasculating the men in our lives as we become more and more successful. We must find the healthy balance between our work, our independence and our womanhood.

My hope is that you will enjoy this book as much as I have enjoyed my journey, while still on it and that you will find some nugget of inspiration to spur you on to live a full, abundant life as you realize your dreams. Real abundant life comes through trusting God in all that we do. While not always as easy as it sounds, through faith, we are able to experience all that God has planned out for us, even when it does not go as planned.

Inside these pages, you will hear stories of faith, encouragement, independence and triumph for women just like you, who have gone down this road.

> "…I (Jesus) have come that they may have life, and have it to the full." (John 10:10 NIV)

Blessings on your journey!

CHAPTER 1 –
YOU'RE FIRED!

So I am no stranger when it comes to work. I actually began working part time at 16 while attending High School, and through my first year of college; manning a snow cone stand to retail athletic stores in the mall. I got my dose of working for a living quite early. At the time, I was not the biggest fan of having to work, but looking back this taught me some important life lessons; lessons I continue to try and teach my own children.

While dating my boyfriend during college, my life took a different turn. As it would turn out, you CAN get pregnant while having sex. Who would have thought, right?! I guess "the talk" didn't really sink in. So the college life was cut short, and REAL life began, a different kind of work. While most would consider this a sad situation, and at times I thought of it that way, and definitely not what my parents or I had planned for myself, I have learned to look at it as a blessing in disguise. I was given an amazing son of whom I am so proud! He was born extremely premature (at 24 weeks) and weighed only 2.2 pounds. There were many reasons he should not be here today, but God intervened and sent him early, and for that I am ever grateful.

In trying to make the best of my situation I started looking for a place of my own. While visiting one of the communities, much to my surprise, I was offered a job. *"You would be great at showing apartments and helping our residents"* the woman said. With such surprise, and not really knowing how to react, I was silent. She added, *"there is a 20% discount on the apartment as part of your salary."* Well, that was enough for me! I moved into a new apartment home, and I began a new job all in the same week, never realizing the path it would lead to. Even though the path was not what I had thought about for myself, I would learn later in life that God was forming my character.

In the years to come, I chose not to finish college, but really excelled at the business I landed in. While education is extremely important, especially in today's day and time, it is possible to be successful among difficult circumstances without a college degree. I am a living example. I urge young people today, and even adults who wish to finish their education, to boldly consider whether it will benefit them or not. Today's graduates finish college with staggering debt, making a salary they could have made without a degree. I understand in many fields it is extremely important, vital even, to your career. College is not for everyone, and it does not take a degree to be successful.

As a youngster of only 23, I had worked my way up from a Part -Time Leasing Consultant to Property Manager, overseeing more than 215 apartment homes and 5 employees, most of them twice my age. I learned some hard and important lessons during those early years. In fact, I probably should have been fired multiple times because of my less than sympathetic nature at the time. It was unacceptable to me for someone to ignore basic rules. "Pay your rent on time or get out" was my motto! Thanks to some fantastic bosses and mentors, I continued to excel. A piece of advice here: seek out mentors, stay close to those who have gone ahead of you and who are successful. They can teach you so much and help you avoid some hard life lessons.

I eventually learned the definition of the word compassion, along with being able to continue to enforce the rules. I learned that you can diffuse a situation with a confident and caring conversation, without having to break a company policy. I learned sometimes people just need an ear for someone to hear them. Many times the solution comes from talking things out.

After learning some important lessons early on, moving up the ladder came fairly easy to me. I had extremely positive parents while growing up and they helped me see anything was possible. I never really saw failure as an option, but that is immaturity at its' finest! As the years went on, I would learn that it takes hard work and determination to make things happen.

In the coming years, I learned how to communicate better, and with a great team around me, I continued to excel with this company. I planned workshops for new employees, trained them on new policies and procedures and introduced them to the company's corporate culture. I provided the tools they needed to begin their journey with their new position. I was blessed to be doing something that truly fit my personality and passions...this is where I believe our purpose from God really shines through, where these qualities intersect.

However, on the home front, two more boys came about. Yes, that makes 3 boys, and in spite of juggling motherhood and being a wife, I would eventually be promoted to a national training position within the company.

Having multiple home and career responsibilities proved to be really difficult. To truly excel at this position and give it all I had, was really not the best option for my family. This formula does not go well together, something eventually will suffer. In fact, my role as a wife was really far down on the list as I drank up the corporate culture of working women and our importance.

If I had some things to do over again, it would be to really understand how important those younger years with my boys were and to truly cherish them. The bottom line is I regret not spending that quality time with them and my priorities were somewhat out of order. However, knowing how merciful and gracious our God is, He has shown me the lessons I learned, and the path I went down, has shaped me into who I am today. He was able to allow me to use the lessons and turn them into blessings.

Take some lessons from my mistakes. Your career can be put on hold if need be. While your kids are young, make and take the time to be with them. If this is why you are looking to start your own business, good for you. I beg you to develop the "why" statement of your business. Make sure you won't be impacting what is important for the wrong reasons.

Life is a journey, and if we don't learn something through all of our mistakes, heartache and pain, it is just an empty existence. My internal being was created specifically for a reason, with many working parts that make me who I am. Psalm 139 says:

"For you created my inmost being; you knit me together in my mother's womb. I praise you because I am fearfully and wonderfully made, your works are wonderful…"

It takes a lifetime to understand and develop those talents and gifts we are given. It takes supportive people in our lives to help develop those talents and gifts. It takes encouragement and time to be the best you can be! And it takes failures and difficult circumstances to really grow through the stages of our lives. As a wise man once said, "change, conflict, growth…"

Because of the conflict my blossoming career was causing, and to spend more time at home with my family, I made some career changes. I knew the software that I trained my employees on like the back of my hand. A headhunter from that software company contacted me to sell their products and it seemed like a good fit. With much thought, and 9 years with a great company, I decided to go into the software sales arena. Even with my training and property management background, sales was a little new for me.

The sales industry is largely relational. I actually did well because I knew the overall property management business and because I do well with people. People do business with people they like… not necessarily because of the product or service you are selling.

During this period in my life, I was dealt some difficult circumstances and in spite of much prayer and counseling for a resolution, my 10 year marriage ended. Needless to say, this took me by surprise, even though as I look back, I can clearly see it shouldn't have, and I was thrown into a new chapter of my life; a chapter of self-discovery, humility and a strengthening and rejuvenation of my faith. I had been fired as a wife.

While this is not a book about relationships, they play a huge part in your success. If you find yourself struggling and juggling life's responsibilities, and you too are a wife, I challenge you to pick up "Love and Respect" by Emerson Eggerichs. This book came in my life a little later than I wished, but it showed me how our husbands are really very simple. Their needs are few, but their biggest need, while you might think is one thing (wink, wink) is really another – RESPECT. Another good one is "The Proper Care and Feeding of Husbands" by Dr. Laura Schlesinger. I won't continue on this topic as I did not intend to write about how to improve as a wife, but I strongly encourage you wives, girlfriends and "wives to be" to make sure you get this in proper perspective, or your marriage might not survive your career.

After only one year with the software company, I had moved on to another opportunity. It just so happens that during this period of time in my life, I was blessed to be working with my father. Unusual circumstances brought my father and me together at the same employer, and thankfully he was there to help me during one of the worst times ever. I honestly do not think I could have endured working every day throughout my separation period had I been working at another job. There were days I just could not function properly and my dad was right there to help me along the way. How amazing is God to have placed my dad in that role, at that time, to help me endure one of the toughest times I have ever had. I will forever be grateful to the Lord for allowing this scenario to happen and to my dad for being there for me during this time.

After working with my dad at this company for the next six years, my steps were redirected again. It is interesting how God places us, and then moves us, even when we are unaware of where we should go. If we would be still and listen more than we try to create our own path, He would direct our steps. I am not saying we sit still and do nothing, but I think at times, we try to plan our way without considering what our purpose and plan in God's will might be.

> *"Be anxious for nothing, but in everything by prayer and petition, with thanksgiving, present your requests to God. And the*

peace of God, which transcends all understanding, will guard your hearts and your minds in Christ Jesus." Philippians 4:6-7

In 2006 my faith and ego were tested again. I felt stale and unhappy. My sales were down and my bosses were looking to me for results, but results just weren't coming. It wasn't because I didn't try, but as I look back, I can see it was truly time for me to take the next step in my journey.

Out of the blue, a recruiter called me to tell me of an available position. He said it fit my background perfectly and he wanted me to interview for it. I was not really interested in another sales position. I truly thought my heart was back in management and training. I wanted to move from a sales mentality back to a management or support role. The recruiter insisted it was a great fit for me, and assured me there would be support in addition to the sales role. I agreed to interview. He was right. It was a perfect fit. Not only did it fit me perfectly based on my background, the employer interviewing me knew many of the same people I knew, and our interview lasted almost 2 hours.

After a second interview with the company's owner, a week later, they offered me the job and I was truly excited. Keep in mind; I still had my current sales position.

The following week I had actually planned to give

my two weeks' notice and leave my current place of employment. It turns out; I was never able to deliver that notice. After multiple times in my younger days of dodging being fired, I had experienced my first termination. It was not pleasant. I got a call from my supervisor informing me he would be on speaker phone with the HR department…not a good sign. After explaining that my performance had suffered lately and my quota had not been met, they were going to have to let me go. Even though I already accepted a position elsewhere, nothing mattered at that moment. I could not believe it! How could they fire me? I had never been fired! What a devastating shot to my ego.

Proverbs 16:18 says "Pride goes before destruction, a haughty spirit before a fall." Haughty – what does that even mean? It means me! I was in this place

disdainfully proud; snobbish; scornfully arrogant

It reminds me that God is in control. We may think we are in control, that we have prestige or power or success, and have things all planned out, but God reminds us that He is truly the one in control.

After the truth sank in, I accepted the fact of what had happened. I was able to look back and understand that the timing was right for this move to happen. In the days to follow I was able to discuss the situation with my family and friends. They helped me to realize the following conclusions and that God was directing my steps while protecting me along the way:

- I would be getting my commissions paid through the next 90 days
- I would be getting my sick and vacation time paid out
- I would be paid my salary through the next 30 days
- AND I would have insurance for the next 90 days for myself and my boys

If I were to have quit as planned, I would not have received any of those perks they offered. I would have given my 2 weeks' notice, and they would have gladly said "Goodbye"; no commissions, no insurance, no nothing!

How was God's plan at work here? I see it. He gently moved me (OK, not so gently) to a better paying position, that fit my skill set even better, with no loss of income or insurance during the transition. He always knows best.

Why is it that sometimes we fail to hear Him? I know for me, I don't listen closely enough. OR, I am already dead set following my own agenda that I fail to recognize the better path He has for me. OR, our pride gets in the way of seeing how our plan is not God's plan.

I love how we can look back on our lives, (they say hind sight is 20/20) and the paths we have taken, and see how God has directed us (if we allow Him) to the greener pasture, or the path that will impact our lives for the better. I can see how he placed each stepping stone from the first day of looking at apartments up to the business I am so fortunate to have today. How awesome is that!

Fast forward 6 years from D-Day (Divorce-Day), and I have experienced a great professional career, created some great relationships, and really excelled at my position. I also earned the most money I had ever made, and it was continuing to grow. I do not attribute this success to myself alone, but I trusted God throughout this time in my life and allowed Him to work it all out.

From the moment of marital separation, I could not wait to get back into the church. What I didn't mention earlier is that I had been a Christian and involved in church since I was about ten years old. All through high school I made good decisions and stayed close to the church and youth group until I hit my twenties. After that I made some bad decisions, went down some crooked paths, and the worst part is I stopped going to church altogether.

In my heart, I also knew I had not been giving back to God. I immediately began bringing the tithe

(10% of my income) to the local church. In spite of financial hardships throughout the beginning of my single parenting days, there was no need that went unmet. The blessings in relationships from my boys to my new church home were worth more than money could buy.

During that last six year run, I met my amazing husband. After being a divorced mother of 3 boys for 7 years, which happens to be God's number of completion interestingly enough, God brought me my life partner in 2009. We knew it was a fit from probably date 2, maybe date 1, but that sounds too unbelievable. We took things very slowly, however. We had both been married before, and we also wanted to make sure our boys (my 3 and his 2) were comfortable before blending our families. We had many similar interests and our faith was the foundation. Meeting at church, and then again through a Christian singles group, we were destined for each other…if you believe in destiny. Ephesians 1:11 says "In Him we were also chosen, having been **predestined** according to the plan of Him who works out everything in conformity with the purpose of His will…". There is that "thing" I mentioned earlier where we get off His track and go down ours to our detriment. God has a perfect plan for our lives, if we would simply hear Him.

This time in my life also reminds me how faithful

God is with not only the tangible, but the intangible… like the love I have received from my husband. He will bless us when we are faithful and obedient. I know I was not always perfect, but God's Word assures us in Psalm 37, that when we *delight in The Lord, He will give us the desires of our heart*. What are your desires?

Chapter 1 Questions to Ponder –

1. Have you thought about your beginning or early years and how far you have come? If you are still in your early years, think about your next steps and know you will experience many ups and downs.

2. What is it that you are passionate about and good at? Painting, cooking, working with children…This is what I believe to be a clue to God's Purpose for your life.

3. When you look back at different times in your life can you see the stepping stones? Even if they are painful, these are the moments that shape us and keep us moving forward.

4. Try to identify some mentors in your life. Who is it that shaped you during the younger years and who can help you today?

5. Define your "why". Define your motivation and goals of what you want to accomplish with your business.

CHAPTER 2 –
FAITH VS. PATIENCE

During our courtship and as we eventually married, my husband kept telling me that I should quit working for someone else and do consulting for myself. I was not sure that is what I wanted to do. I liked my job, but I wasn't sure I could see myself doing it forever.

My husband encouraged me constantly, and praised the work I did. He gave me confidence every day, and eventually convinced me that I could actually make my own business work. We made prayer a priority and sought advice from many counselors. Proverbs 15:22 says "Plans fail for lack of counsel, but with many advisers they succeed." We sought out successful friends and family members who started their own businesses many years ago, as well as those who weren't so successful, to find out what to do, and what not to do.

One such counselor we sought was a close friend that has a successful financial consulting company and part of his experience entails analyzing business opportunities. As it would happen my husband and this friend had a desire to find the right business of their own. During a review of my business, he felt I had a good business model and he wanted in. He highly encouraged this business opportunity between the three of us. After 20 years of my husband and friend searching for their joint business opportunity, they felt this was a venture they both could truly support. The keen financial and business sense made him a great partner. The three of us were ready to roll!

Understand that when you are sharing your dreams and visions with those closest to you, they may not all be on your side. In fact, they may THINK they are on your side, but due to THEIR fears and insecurities, their advice could be negative, and possibly hinder your plans.

It was so interesting that our closest Christian friends and family gave us many good things to think about, and they were not simply jumping on the "start your own business bandwagon". In fact, they could not really understand why I would give up my six figure income for the unknown, and the possibility of failure. Much less, they could not fathom my husband joining me in the future, foregoing his six figure income as well. After all, isn't that the American Dream today - to make as much money as possible?

After all the prayer and discussion, we eventually made the decision to go for it and start the business. With me as the face and feet of the company, it was a scary but exciting time for us. Our partner led us through all the steps to set up our business entity. As a business consultant, he was able to handle the paperwork and set up the business quicker than I had imagined. Within 30 days we were on our way.

It is critical to know your limitations and timeline. Without the right partners, you either pay for knowledge or increase time to gain it.

The MaRK Advantage was born January 1, 2012. It could not have happened without my wonderful husband spurring me on. Proverbs 31:11 says "Her husband has full confidence in her and lacks nothing of value." We will talk further about those of you who are unmarried or feel you have no supporting partner, but to those of you with a partner like mine, consider yourself blessed by a loving, supportive husband. Realize he can help you reach new heights that you never thought you could reach on your own.

In the months to come, I was responsible for getting the business going. My husband actually kept his day job and our plan was to get to a certain point with clients and income, before he would quit. The determination we made was from my past experience and my partner's consulting experience. Once we had approximately 40,000 apartment units under our consulting umbrella, my husband would join the business full time.

Because of my relationships over the past 15 years, I was able to build a strong supplier network to get our business off the ground. I had relationships with people who were truly excited that I would be on my own. I had a great start and was truly blessed to be venturing out on my own!

Even with strong relationships I chose to start from scratch as it relates to new clients. I left on good terms from the old job, and promised I would start a business with integrity and character. I wanted to keep my promise, and I did.

As the months passed by, the business should have been further along, but I felt like I was somewhat stuck and stagnant. We had some good clients and the income was fair, but certainly not enough to replace what I had given up.

Our thoughts and prayers kept coming back around to "do we have faith?" or "do we need patience?" What I mean by this is, did we need faith for my husband to take the plunge, or did we just need patience to hang in there until we got enough clients to sustain our income? As a reminder, we set a goal before he would quit. That goal was based on comfort income.

Our level of faith had already been strengthened throughout this process, as we continued to tithe on both of our previous incomes, even though I was not receiving a check anymore. We wanted to continue to give at the same level, and trust that God would replace it.

Eight months into the business, at morning coffee, my husband and I felt the strong desire that it was time for him to quit his corporate job of 13 years. The constant prayer and guidance we had been seeking had seemed to pay off with an answer. But we were not exactly sure how we could survive on such a low income if he were to quit. We calculated what we had saved, and decided how we would live in a bare bones situation. We figured with our savings, we could at least live about a year, to a year and a half, even if we made nothing.

The business was making some money, so we knew we would have our needs met, barring no major surprises. In fact, when thinking of starting your own business, at least six month's living expenses saved is good, but more like a year's is ideal. I would bet most people don't even know what their true living expenses are. We tend to think of cable television and multiple vehicles as needs, when in fact, they are not. You would be surprised what you can live without.

After our morning discussion, and the talk about

leaving the day job, we both had a peace about the decision that we never had before. The Lord kept reassuring us, with various scripture and with various people that spoke into our lives, that this was the time to make our move. Our trust was in our bank account and not in our Heavenly Father. After we realized the trust was in money and gave that up, we had such a peace from God. There is no other feeling like releasing your cares to Him!

Our faith has released God's power. That was our new motto…we were about to walk on water. We were not sure if our business would succeed, but we knew for sure that God wanted us to make a move in obedience. In our actions, he would prove to be faithful, but in what way? We were not sure.

This was probably one of the most exciting times in my life. Exciting and a little nerve racking, but only because of the unknown. Fear of the unknown will keep you stuck in the same place day after day. Let go and let God, as they say. You will find a power you never knew existed. Just having the faith of a mustard seed will prove to be enough. Our God is big and His Word promises that if we seek Him with all our heart, mind and soul, He will give us the desires of our heart. We were cashing in on His promises. We could not wait to see what God was going to do with us and our business. Better yet, how He would use our story to change others' lives and be a testimony for our faith.

Most of us aren't confident or courageous. Most of us are flat out scared to death. We're afraid to take risks, afraid of failure, and afraid of dying. We're not walking confidently because we're not people of faith.

Do you want to be a person of faith? Faith is God's Word activated. The Bible says in Romans 10:17, *"Faith comes from hearing the message and the message is heard through the Word about Christ"* (NIV).

If you've ever read a verse in the Bible and all of a sudden thought, "I can do this! I can do this!" you've just had your faith activated by the Word of God.

Now don't be fooled, we did not make a rushed move overnight. We made plans, consulted in others, weighed all the negativity given to us, and we also saved our money. We prepared our fields, as you might say, for the rains to come.

Are you ready to move? Let God move you. Do not let fear stand in the way of God's plan for your life. He will take care of the daily needs when we have just the faith of a mustard seed. Trust Him and see what will happen!

Even after a year in business our rain had not

come as we thought it would, but we knew the needs would be provided for. And by taking that first step, it allowed us to be that much more open when God called us to the next step.

"Your heavenly Father already knows perfectly well what you need and He will give it to you if you give Him first place in your life and live as He wants you to." (Matthew 6:33 LB)

Our goal was not to simply make money. As my sweet sister and my brother - in - law taught us, ***freedom and time*** are what drives us. We know the blessings will come, financially, spiritually and in many other ways, money just can't touch.

In fact, we also know that God could have been using the step of faith with starting the business and leaving our corporate jobs to break our ties of trust in money. We anticipated great things knowing they could go well beyond what our new business would do.

Matthew 6:11 says "give us today our daily bread…" It does not say please provide for us, it says GIVE! This says to me that The Lord already plans to provide for our needs (maybe not all our wants, but definitely our needs). We don't even have to ask. We do not have to worry about whether He will take care of our daily needs, He will!

This does not mean that we will never feel fear

again, or worry, but once you take the leap of faith, you realize your God is bigger than any need you will ever have. And keep in mind; our "needs" do not always match up with God's idea of "needs". Many times our wants are misinterpreted as needs. He will provide all you need!

Chapter 2 Questions to Ponder –

1. Where are you in the business birthing process?
2. Do you have your faith in money or in God?
3. How will you handle the negativity from those around you when it comes?
4. Have you prepared for the rain?

CHAPTER 3 –
ANGELA: A CASE STUDY OF FAITH

ANGELA - Angela grew up in a blended family, very similar to the Brady Bunch. Her mother had 3 children and her step-father had 3 children. From a young age Angela became very independent, as most children from a large family do. She was used to doing things herself and in many ways grew up too fast. At age 12 she began smoking, and by age 17, the doctor told her she had the worst lungs he had ever seen in a teen!

Because of her doctor report, Angela began learning as much about nutrition and health as she possibly could. She found she really had a passion for learning about the body and how it worked at its maximum potential. Not to mention she knew she had to make some serious changes to stay healthy.

After getting her Associates degree, Angela pursued a career in the corporate world. She worked herself tirelessly from an administrative assistant to a marketing manager after a senior executive noticed her drive. However, Angela's passion continued in nutrition. But it was after the birth of her child when she realized she loved pediatric nutrition and learning about the health and well-being of children.

As a self-proclaimed poor student of math and science, Angela never thought she would be able to move from marketing to nutritionist because of the schooling required. But she was determined to see if her dream could become a reality. She enrolled in school to obtain the classes she needed to become a Registered Dietitian. To her surprise, she was a straight A student! Her advice: never forego trying something because of a preconceived notion.

In 2008, Angela started her own nutrition private practice while holding her current position as a clinical dietitian at a pediatric hospital. But by 2009, she felt it was time to take the plunge and go "all in". She started her private practice and has never looked back. This is what Angela had to say when we sat down together.

> M: *Obviously, you have been passionate about nutrition for a long time, but what was the catalyst in your decision to start your own business?*

A: My new family. After growing up with parents who worked constantly, I didn't want my kids to be in the same situation. I also knew my faith in God was my first priority, with family second. I wanted the freedom to keep those things a priority as well as build a company that shared these values while serving others.

M: *Talk about some of the support you had around you. Who was your "cheerleader" in the beginning?*

A: My husband. He is actually our CFO and takes care of many aspects of the business. Also, it was critical for me that we each saw it as our business, not just my business. My Home Team from my church was also encouraging. Our small group of friends continued to cover us in prayer as we stepped out in faith to make this business decision. As we prayed, I would move forward step by step in faith. Although it took a while for our business to create good, consistent income – it was clear that I was headed in the right direction. Things were happening.

M: *Have you ever second guessed your decision?*

A: I'll be honest, yes. It takes time to make money, and once we made money, we would sink it back into the business. In the beginning, it kept me wondering if we had made the right decision. But now that we're into our 5th year and we've added 2 new employees that have assisted in growing the business as well – things are now really hopping. If I would've given up early on, I would not have gotten here. Our pastor at church says that chaos usually precedes growth. That has been true with our business. Before I was able to add headcount, I had to do everything myself. We had to get to a point in the business that we could justify adding people to the business. So during that time it was really hard. But I am so glad I stuck with it! It is now paying off nicely.

M: *Are you at the level of success you thought you would be at this point in your journey?*

A: I think I have exceeded it. I measure success not only financially but by other blessings as well. Every day I see a child or an adult for nutrition issues and they leave with hope, guidance and support – that is true satisfaction. I make people healthier using food as medicine, whether it is to help someone heal or to prevent a disease. Either way, the potential to impact someone's life is substantial. No amount of money gives you that satisfaction. My passion for others has driven me to become a media spokesperson for 75,000 dietitians all over the world. I felt lead to apply for a position that not many get in my industry. It has helped provide me with name exposure and boosted my career, more than I could ever imagine. I acknowledge it is not due to anything special I have done, but what God has done through me. He has plans that are so much bigger than me, and I am just grateful to be playing a part!

M: *What is the most difficult thing about having your own business?*

A: You are never off. I could turn off my day job before, knowing tomorrow I would start over. But with my own business, especially in the beginning, it was just me.

M: *What is the best thing?*

A: To be able to make a difference in others'

lives. I also value being able to change directions as I feel led and being able to make my own decisions for the benefit of each patient.

M: *If doing it all over, would you do everything the same way?*

A: Yes, no looking back. Everything that we have been through has lead us to where we are now.

M: *At what point do you consider yourself successful?*

A: When I feel I am making a difference. Now – every day!

Angela Lemond is a Registered Dietitian and the current Director-at-Large, Communications for the Texas Academy of Nutrition and Dietetics and a national spokesperson for the Academy of Nutrition and Dietetics. She is the co-owner of Lemond Nutrition and lives happily in Allen, TX with her husband, Jeff, also co-owner and CFO, and their two children.

CHAPTER 4 – GETTING INTO THE GAME / BEING A PROVERBS 31 WOMAN

What are your dreams? What are your desires? I like to think of our dreams and desires as a link to the purpose God has for our lives. Do you have ideas that just never come to fruition because you don't think anyone will appreciate them or listen to you? Many times as I was writing this book, I would hear myself say "Why are you writing a book?" "No one cares what you have to say." "Who are YOU to be writing a book on encouragement?" I had to constantly stand on the promises of God, knowing He had a plan and a purpose for my life beyond my wildest imagination. I felt that included telling my story and sharing words of encouragement with other women.

Consider the influence of the Proverbs 31 woman. The writer of this Proverb, I believe, was showing all the mighty influences and skills of a woman. I don't believe this woman did everything all at one time (whew!), no one could live up to that, but I do believe the example is to show us all the amazing gifts and talents that God gave to women to help us realize our purpose. Let's look a little closer to see what we think the author is trying to share.

The dictionary defines the word *noble* as *"possessing high ideals or excellent moral character,"* while the word character is defined as *"the set of qualities that make someone distinctive, especially in qualities of mind and feeling."*

> *She selects wool and flax and works with eager hands.* (Prov 31:13 NIV)

To me, this says she is not afraid to gather the raw materials and create, sew and work with her hands. This means we have to get into the game. We are not created to simply sit on the sidelines and cheer others on, although some of us are gifted at that. God created us unique and special. We have abilities to create and work. Working is a great thing. It allows us to make a difference in the world which is why we are on this planet.

> *She is like the merchant ships, bringing her food from afar.* (Prov 31:14 NIV)

Not only does the P31 woman work with her

hands, she travels and plans to bring in food for her family or for herself. It is with careful thought and preparation that she goes about her day.

She gets up while it is still night. (Prov 31:15 NIV)

Some of us may struggle with this one, but getting up early and taking on the day truly does allow for success. Whether you are feeding your family a good breakfast to begin their day, having your quiet time or jumping into your work, prioritizing is the key. I find that getting into my day early, not only gives me a head start on my projects, but it allows me to finish earlier. Balance is a very important element of being successful. Getting to work early, getting the tasks done, finishing early and having time for other things is a great perk to having your own business.

She provides food for her family and portions for her female servants. (Prov 31:15b NIV)

Providing food for your family is one thing, but also for your servants, that is quite another. This speaks to the kind hearted woman she is. Let's not lose sight of how we can continually make a difference by reaching out to others, not only our own families, but those in need. Serving allows us to get outside of ourselves and pour into others to fill a need. It is essential, in my opinion, of living a balanced life.

She considers a field and buys it; out of her earnings she plants a vineyard. (Prov 31:16 NIV)

This speaks of the knowledge women have to buy…real estate, businesses, stocks, etc. Women have the resources today to truly educate themselves. Not only does she have the knowledge of what to buy, she makes it profitable by planting a vineyard…notice she did not plant grain, but a *vineyard*…we DO need a glass of Merlot every now and then! Out of her earnings she plants the vineyard…it takes money to make money and this woman is a savvy businesswoman.

She sets about her work vigorously; her arms are strong for her tasks. (Prov 31:17 NIV)

I truly think this speaks to our balance between work and health. Vigorously means balance between mental and physical strength. Her arms are strong for her tasks, but also her mind. If we don't take care of ourselves and keep our bodies and minds healthy and strong we are no good to anyone, especially ourselves. Make sure you set aside time, even schedule it if necessary, to work out your body and keep your body in good working order. Keep your mind sharp and alert by continuous learning and reading. Our lives should be a continual journey of bettering ourselves and don't forget that our bodies are a temple.

She sees that her trading is profitable (Prov 31:18 NIV)

Without trying to sound too "women's libbish", I feel the writer is talking about how smart we really are when it comes to our finances. It used to be that men were the Wall Street gurus and women really did not have a place in the market. Many women are holding high profile positions, as well as making more money than ever before. The P31 woman ensures she spends wisely, invests wisely and always tries to ensure a profit. As we know, there are risks involved with trading, so making sure we are knowledgeable is a must. Or we must hire a knowledgeable firm to assist with trading if we are unsure how to do it ourselves.

and her lamp does not go out at night. (Prov 31:18b NIV)

This verse could be interpreted to mean that even in the darkness, a woman of virtue still finds things to do in the home. As they say, "a woman's work is never done". Or you could interpret this for married women in reference to pleasing your man. For some of you, this might make you cringe, but it is a gift that we can give to our husbands, as well as a gift to ourselves. Our lamps may be flickering, but they should stay lit until our husbands are satisfied. The Bible tells us "our bodies are not our own" and for us married women, we are one with our spouses, making sure they are taken care of. Trust me; this is one of the keys to a long lasting marriage.

In her hand she holds the distaff and grasps the spindle with her fingers. (Prov 31:19 NIV)

Yet another analogy regarding working with our hands. There are so many ways we were made to contribute to this world and working with our hands to make things is such a blessing bestowed to us. We don't count it valuable enough because I think so many women don't realize their full potential in how they were created. I think these days, women never even scratch the surface of the things they can do. Try new things; find out what you like to do with your hands. Is it sewing, needlepoint, scrapbooking, arts and crafts…?

She opens her arms to the poor and extends her hands to the needy. (Prov 31:20 NIV)

This is an area where I think as women we exceed our male counterparts. Our hearts are compassionate and for most of us this comes very easy. We are made to think of others with compassion and to help those less fortunate. Do you have a cause you are passionate about? If not, think on it a while and you will find it. Most likely it is in your pain. The wounds we endure end up being our ministry. Once you find it, make a concerted effort to give back on behalf of this cause. Is it the poor, or is it the orphan, is it the battered woman? You know what it is. Many times it is the very thing that you suffered from or experienced in your past. Uphold our Father's expectation and act upon that need that you are passionate about.

> *When it snows, she has no fear for her household; for all of them are clothed in scarlet.*
> (Prov 31:21 NIV)

The New Living Translation interprets this verse to say; for all of them have warm clothes. What this says to me is that the family will not be cold or go unattended. The P31 woman has full faith in her Lord that her household will be cared for. This is a big step for us. It is difficult, especially for single women, to comprehend and keep that faith that we will be cared for. We must trust our Lord that whether single or married, we will have no fear in winter, for our household will be clothed in warm clothes and fully provided for. Being prepared is also present to me in this verse. We must prepare for those times that may be cold, or difficult. I don't think we only have to have faith and things will turn out fine, I think we have to prepare, as well as have that faith, so things may go in our favor.

She makes coverings for her bed; she is clothed in fine linen and purple. (Prov 31:22 NIV)

The P31 woman is at it again, making coverings for her bed. Whether we make them, buy them, or simply accept something given to us, we make sure our bed is our resting place. We make sure we get adequate rest and understand our bed can be our refuge.

Not only do we make our bed our refuge, but we clothe ourselves in fine linen and purple. Back in the day, purple was the color of royalty. Ladies, we are daughters of the King, which makes us royalty. Never forget to take pride in your appearance, no matter what you are doing, and clothe yourself accordingly. This is not saying to be materialistic and spend all your money on the most expensive fashions, but it is saying we take pride in how we dress. We will be taken more seriously when we dress in a modern and professional manner in the workplace. Not only in the workplace, but for those of us working from home, we need to make sure we get dolled up for ourselves, and our husbands, periodically. It is a proven fact that "when you look good, you feel good *dahling*!"

Her husband is respected at the city gate, where he takes his seat among the elders of the land. (Prov 31:23 NIV)

Some of us are married, some of us are not.

The fact is, those people in our lives should be respected and engaged in the community and the local church. For those of us who are married, it is a testament to our "picking" skills and knowing who God has for us. If we chose correctly, our husband will be respected and highly thought of. Think on this if you are unmarried. Those who you are considering dating, or think might be marriage material, what do others think of him? Do others look up to him? Call him for advice? This is more important than you might think. Consider his reputation and willingness to help others. If your husband is less than meeting this criteria, there is always hope. God can change people and by a Godly example of a woman, a man can be changed. But before saying "I do", you will want to decide if this is the type of husband you really want.

> *She makes linen garments and sells them, and supplies the merchants with sashes.* (Prov 31:24 NIV)

A Super Saleswoman! Not only is she making garments, but she sells them. She is smart and she has people skills. There is no doubt about how God has instilled our abilities to make clothing, or other things, and to earn a good living because of that. Our purpose from God is not to be taken lightly, regardless of what our occupations end up being.

She is clothed with strength and dignity; she can laugh at the days to come. (Prov 31:25 NIV)

Strength and dignity... To me, that does not say we have no say so, or we have to ask permission for something. We have been given an inherent strength to be able to make decisions for our household and beyond. We should have a high self-esteem and respect for ourselves as this is how we were created. The second part of this verse says we can have a sense of humor. This is an important quality for us to be able to move forward. If we don't laugh, accept and enjoy each present moment, we will focus on the mistakes or failures of the past as well as be fearful of the future. We can also focus on our aging and changing bodies and faces to where our focus gets off track. Poke fun at your wrinkles and sagging areas...laugh or you might cry!

She speaks with wisdom, and faithful instruction is on her tongue. (Prov 31:26 NIV)

A wise woman continues her learning in the Word and otherwise, and is not afraid to share her wisdom with others. This is especially important in the lives of other women. We are called to share with others. By giving instruction to those younger than us we are able to help save them from the mistakes we made... possibly. We have to at least try!

> *She watches over the affairs of her household and does not eat the bread of idleness.*
> (Prov 31:27 NIV)

It is easy for us to watch over the affairs of our household, but eat the bread of idleness?? I don't know about you, but I have been known to eat a loaf or two of that in the past. Having said that, making good use of all our time is so critical. Planning and moving forward with your household or your business is a key to success. No one ever made anything of themselves by sitting idle. Keep tabs on yourself. Naps here and there are very important in recharging your batteries, but keep it in check. The flip side of that is important to keep track of as well. Staying so busy with the good, that the best passes you by is just as dangerous. Keep your balance.

> *Her children arise and call her blessed; her husband also, and he praises her:* (Prov 31:28 NIV)

I don't think my children have actually arisen and called me blessed, but I know they appreciate the things I have done. I have received a thank you from them every now and then for putting their needs first. It is also nice when the husband praises us for those things we do. Sure, many times we are expected to have their dinner made when they are done with work, but it is also a choice. It is a give and take. As we give, and they show their appreciation, we want to give more. As my husband praises me, it encourages me to want to "up the giving" to another level. The book "Love & Respect" reminds me that when the wife's need of being loved is met, she is able to give her husband the respect he desires. This keeps the "energizing cycle" alive!

> *"Many women do noble things, but you surpass them all." Charm is deceptive, and beauty is fleeting; but a woman who fears the Lord is to be praised. Honor her for all that her hands have done, and let her works bring her praise at the city gate.* (Prov 31:29-30 NIV)

This Proverb is a wonderful ending to this section. This is our goal and should be our motto. Women are a beautiful and amazing creation. Our hands continue to do good works and every day we have the ability to change the world. But the most important thing to take away from this chapter is our faith and "fear" of The Lord. This is not a scary fear but a healthy fear. Understanding and proclaiming The Lord is to be praised, and trusting He gave you all you need to live out your dreams!

Chapter 4 Questions to Ponder:

1. Without feeling inferior to the Proverbs 31 woman (remember no woman can live up to the entire P31 woman), what areas do you need to focus on to help you achieve the next level?

2. How can these traits propel you within the business world or with your ministry?

3. Write down 3 things you can do this week to improve your standing as a Proverbs 31 woman.

CHAPTER 5 –
GOALS – THE WRITTEN WORD

How do you know if your business will be profitable? When will you consider yourself successful? These questions have to be answered prior to getting your business going or you will not know what you are working towards or how to gauge your success. Simply having your own business is great, but unless you are doing it on the side, your goal is to make a profit. The only way you will know when this happens is to understand what it takes from the very beginning.

One of the first steps of considering a business is creating a formal business plan. There are simple templates available on the web to help you create this plan. Any partner, investor or lender will require this before considering any outlay of money to assist you and your new business, if you will need assistance.

Part of your business plan will be what it will take to be a profitable business. This will include what expenses you plan to incur, purchases for startup and the revenue you believe you will generate over your first year and beyond. This is the start of your written plan and ultimate goal.

After you have put your business plan together, secured any financing you may need and prepare to open shop, you will want to think about how you will achieve your short term goals. This will include your daily and weekly plans, as well as your monthly and quarterly goals. Questions will need to be answered such as how many touch points does it take to get a conversation started, which will lead to a proposal and a sale? Or how many customers do I need to have walking through my door in order to make a sale?

I remember, when I was about 27 years old, working in my corporate training job, I was making about $50K per year, plus bonuses. Not too shabby at that time, but nevertheless, my goal, as is most young professionals even today, was to earn 6 figures. I had learned the value of goal setting and putting my goals in writing early on, so I decided to put this to the test. I put together a short list of personal and professional goals of mine which included making $100K annually. For this goal, my only mistake was not putting a time frame on it. I saved the document and continued on with my work, not thinking of this particular exercise for a while. However, subconsciously, this goal was infused in my brain. My foreshadowing of this accomplishment was not constantly on my mind, but it played a big part in the way I made decisions from that point forward. In fact, even today, 15 years later, I remember exactly where I was when I wrote that goal down and can picture the whole scene.

This concept is actually taken right out of scripture. In the book of Habakkuk you remember that the majestic God is in control of your life, no matter what happens to you.

> *And then God answered: "Write this. Write what you see. Write it out in big block letters so that it can be read on the run. This vision-message is a witness pointing to what's coming. It aches for the coming—it can hardly wait! And it doesn't lie. If it seems slow in coming, wait. It's on its way. It will come right on time."*
> (Habakkuk 2:2-3 – MSG)

It probably took me at least a good five years to actually accomplish that goal, but regardless of the time frame, I did it. And in fact, when I had realized my accomplishment, I thought back to the day that I put it in writing and expected it to come to fruition. The next goal had to be to increase my income each year, which, with the exception of the recession in 2008, I had done.

Listen to the power of the written word from Jim Carrey:

"I wrote myself a check for ten million dollars for acting services rendered and dated it Thanksgiving 1995. I put it in my wallet and it deteriorated. And then, just before Thanksgiving 1995, I found out I was going to make ten million dollars for Dumb & Dumber. I put that check in the casket with my father because it was our dream together."

Jim Carrey, The Oprah Winfrey Show 1997

Today, my goals for myself are much more meaningful than simply how much money I can make, as I have learned the quality of life and time with my family and friends are worth more than any amount of money can buy. But the point is we have to know what our goals are. And we have to go one step further in writing them down and looking, thinking and reviewing them frequently.

Some key points to consider when goal setting are as follows:

DETAILED - Make sure to write your goals out in complete detail. What you want, how you will get there, and who will help you achieve the goal, are major factors in actually realizing your goals and dreams.

POSITIVE - Keep your goals written in a positive format, rather than a negative. By keeping in mind what you want to accomplish, not what you want to leave behind, is a powerful way of thinking. For example, your goal is to leave your day job for the dream of your own business. You will write down "open my own bakery…" and not simply to stop working for someone else…. Of course you will elaborate on your goals and how you will get there, but this keeps your mental state focused on your specific dreams, and not what you do want to leave behind. It keeps it positive.

REALISTIC - Keep these goals realistic. I have learned, by being in sales for many years, that if my goals are unrealistic I will be disappointed - A LOT. I will let myself down because I am a believer in meeting and exceeding expectations, including my own. Make sure your financial goals are realistic, and make sure your plans in achieving those goals are also realistic. Do not write down things that you "hope" for. It is fine to reach for the stars, but make sure you understand what the reality really is.

ANALYZE - Currently, I have a goal that is actually lower than what I began the year with. Do not be afraid to adjust your goals as you see fit. If things are not going as you originally planned, make some adjustments before you leave yourself disappointed with the entire outcome. Do not allow yourself to sandbag your goals and dreams, but keep them realistic, and as you focus, make any adjustments necessary due to the economy, unexpected happenings, etc. Make all changes to your written plan so you are always aware of what you need to do.

Every time you make a decision during the day, ask yourself this question, "Does it take me closer to, or further from my goal." If the answer is "closer to," then you've made the right decision. If the answer is "further from," well, you know what to do.

If you follow this process every day you will be on your way to achieving unlimited success in every aspect of your life.

Chapter 5 Questions to Ponder:

1. Do I already have my goals written down? Short term and long term. If not, now is the time. Take time before the next chapter and write down your goals.

2. Am I keeping these goals at the forefront of my every day decision making, and if not, how can I make changes to ensure that I do?

3. Are my goals detailed, positive and realistic? Are they accurate and up to date? Make any changes necessary.

4. Set BIG Goals! Go ahead. Take some more time and jot down some things that may seem unrealistic and farfetched. Seal them up and put them somewhere you can find and open later. You will be surprised!

CHAPTER 6 –
LEAD GENERATION

So we have the desire, and we have the drive. We have our goals written down and in place. We know we were created by God with unique gifts and talents to do great things. We have a vision of our own business but where do we find the new clients, how do we get the orders coming? How do we get started?

Do you have a company name? Do you have a catchy slogan? Have you ordered business cards? If not, you will want to think about your business, how it will operate, store front, internet? Chances are you have many of these questions answered by this stage in the game.

"What's next? How do we gain clients? What was my next step?" Lots of new questions running through my mind and anxiety setting in, wondering if this was really going to work and what have I gotten myself into!? In addition to the questions I had, I had promised the organization I left that I would not directly solicit their clients. Since I started a similar consulting business, I wanted to make sure that I kept my integrity as well as a good relationship with the people I worked with for six years. All of a sudden, I went from multiple clients and multiple projects to zero clients and zero projects and I had to start from scratch.

From my sales background, I knew I had to create a target list. In the book "Ultimate Sales Machine" by Chet Holmes, he advises to create your "Dream List". Who are the companies you want to work with? Where are they? Who are the contact people? What is their email or phone number? I took all this information into consideration and started my target list. Of course, I started in my own backyard of Dallas/Ft. Worth, but I also reached out to other markets. My company can service anyone nationwide, so all markets were really open season to add to my target list.

For me this came so easy. As I talked with others, it was like they had never thought about a target list or where the clients would come from as I had, but this is a very important first step in the business process. It takes time and thought. Who is your target audience? Where is your target market? I started with a simple Excel spreadsheet listing potential customer name, city, contact person, email and phone.

The internet is an amazing wealth of information these days. It takes time to really dig into the information and find what you need, but it can be done. From social media sites, which we will talk about later in Chapter 11, to simple online yellow pages and search sites, we can find just about any and all types of leads and prospects. I spent days just trolling the internet looking for real estate and property management companies in the areas I was looking to target. Nothing was too great or too small, but there was a limit to the prospects I added to my list. Our target market was a certain size company. It did not make sense to add companies that did not fit our target size. As my list grew, my confidence grew. I knew I had a story to tell and these are the people I would tell that story to.

In Chet Holmes' book, The Ultimate Sales Machine, as I previously mentioned, he speaks about your Dream List. Creating a dream client list is envisioning the future before it happens. Will you sell to all the clients on your Dream List? Probably not, but this is how we gain our vision. This is where you get your start. Not only do you continue working through your Dream List for as long as possible, you add to it as needed. As you find prospects that are just not a fit for your company, you will drop them from your list. You will need to replace these clients to make sure you have enough prospecting in your pipeline.

Proverbs 29:18 says "Where there is no vision

the people perish." Make sure you keep your vision in the forefront.

For my purposes, I used an Excel spreadsheet with columns for company name, contact name, size of company, as well as contact information. I color coded to stay organized and motivated. I used green shading at the top to represent dollar signs. They were signed and current clients. The blue were very good prospects that were currently in the works and the probability of closing was very high over the next 90 days. The orange were contacts that had been made and progress was moving forward, but very slowly. The probability of closing on them was much less, either because of lack of communication on their part, or it was not a priority to them. However, I was hopeful these would turn into clients at some point or another.

The yellow represented contact made but no real progress yet and red represented dead prospects. These were prospects that would not become clients. This is just one way to go about it and my list was quite lengthy. I created it that way because the sales cycle is such a long process at times. There are the top prospects you want to communicate with often to stay in front of and press on to closing, and then there are others you will reach out to on a somewhat regular basis to generate more interest that will take you to a call or meeting point. Once that happens they move from yellow to orange, and so on.

You must keep this list open daily to keep your focus on your targets and always be thinking of how you can stay in front of them to generate interest until such time as you close on them. When in sales, the process can be slow and frustrating. You will need to keep yourself positive and motivated. You might even have to adjust your marketing efforts on a regular basis.

There are multiple resources you can use to manage your contacts and clients, but in the beginning, to save money, I would suggest utilizing a spreadsheet or other simple inexpensive way to keep track of your progress. Once you have some money coming in you might want to invest in a software program that will make keeping track of sales and prospects much easier.

If you have an online presence you will have multiple ways to create leads. Make sure to create a blog and post often. We will touch on this more under social media as well. On your website, you will want as much information as possible to create interest. You must have a spot for inquiries. These will become your leads as well, so add them to your spreadsheet or other method of contact.

Don't have an online presence or website? You might want to reconsider. Many people may not find your business online, but they will certainly look to see if it is a valid business after speaking with you or getting an email. Sometimes this is a critical component of validating a business. Websites today are extremely affordable and well worth the cost.

If you are just starting out, Excel will work fine, but as you grow, or if you want to invest early in contact management, ACT or Salesforce.com are both great tools to track leads from inception to close. You can also track any type of contacts for those businesses who are not sales driven.

Utilizing a blog, social media outlets and online or paper newsletters will keep you in front of your audience and generate leads or referrals. Continue to modify your marketing plan to include as many touch points as possible.

Keep in mind; you can't do everything, especially if you are a company of one. Pick a few areas of focus and don't worry about the rest. As you grow, you can have other employees focus on lead tracking as well.

Chapter 6 Questions to Ponder –

1. How do you generate leads today? Consider a Dream List.

2. Do you have a good tracking system or could you make some improvements?

3. Could you enhance your marketing program to give you more visibility and generate more leads?

CHAPTER 7 – PERSEVERING THROUGH THE PROCESS

"No" **is a** hard word to accept when you are talking about your own personal business. Even harder to accept is when you hear nothing. Why can't people just communicate?? They don't have time, it is not a good fit, or they just don't like my Texas accent!! Unfortunately, we have to have thick skin when building our business because it becomes very personal. At least I know it did for me. Fortunately, my previous sales experience taught me that I would not hear "yes" every time. And at times I would never hear anything.

I had developed somewhat of a thicker skin, but each and every time I got a "no" or worse yet, silence, I had to go back to the drawing board and remember the fact that "good things come to those who wait"… or better yet "persevere"!

per·se·ver·ance - [pur-s*uh*-**veer**-*uh*ns]

noun - <u>**steady**</u> persistence in a course of action, a purpose, a state, etc., especially ***in spite of difficulties, obstacles, or discouragement***.

This is a word you need to become very familiar with, if you haven't already.

<u>Steady</u>. This means even during the times that you don't feel like working that day, or don't want to hear "no" again; you keep your course of action. That is the key to your success. The difficulties, obstacles and discouragement will all come, trust me. But that is OK. It is important to be prepared for those times by understanding they will come. How do you prepare for this? You simply acknowledge that the road to success will not be easy. You know it takes hard work and determination. Prepare your mind for the difficult times; know they will come and accept them. You will also be quick to recognize how you need to trust in God to keep going. In His timing, the success will come.

Keeping a strong support system around you is critical. We will address this more in Chapter 14, **Networking**, but family and friends are a critical component when venturing out on your own.

If you are single, make sure you keep your close knit group of friends near you during the good times as well as the tough times. At least one or 2 close friends is ideal. Use them to bounce ideas off of, as well as to receive and give encouragement. Having a church home is also extremely helpful. By plugging in to areas at your local church you will draw from support all around you, not to mention have multiple opportunities to share your story with others, and even pick up a client or sale in the process. Check out your singles department at your church. Staying close to your local church home also brings benefits of strengthening your faith that you might not even expect.

For those married ladies, or those with significant others, make sure to lean on them, but do not overwhelm them with all the details and discouragement. They can be a huge resource to encourage, but don't forget they probably have jobs too and they will stop listening if you never ask about them. The saying "It's not all about you", is hard to admit but true!

While having a support team around you via friends and family is critical, the main component in persevering through the process, however, is YOU. Your attitude and work ethic will determine your success.

I have seen multiple people start their own businesses only to think it gives them freedom to do less work. While in the long run, after your business is successful, this can be true, but in the beginning this could not be farther from the truth. You have to put in the extra hours and the extra effort. You have to communicate more and hustle more. Depending on your business model, you may have to travel more or be out in the field more. It will create stress for you and for those around you, but persevere.

Your faith will be strengthened because you will be forced to trust in The Lord more in the beginning. If you believe He will provide for you, and you are doing all you can to make that happen, He will. Do not be anxious for anything....He has your back.

Another thing to keep in mind as you are persevering through the process is to make sure to stay balanced. We can tend to start working first thing in the morning and continue on until late in the evening and even on weekends.

The real key to your balance is to ensure you keep the key elements in check:

- ✓ Spiritual
- ✓ Health
- ✓ Relationships
- ✓ Rest

We touched on staying involved in your local church and this is so important. Keep your faith strengthened by staying in His Word and talking to

The Lord continuously. He is the source of all our hope. You must keep this in the forefront of your mind as you grow your business. God's plans are not always our plans. Keep His plans in mind and allow them to take priority over your plans, even when it feels painful.

If you don't eat right and exercise you won't have the physical strength to endure all you need to endure with your business. There will be long days, and depending on the nature of your business, exhausting days, mentally and physically. Staying away from fast food and eating an adequate number of fruits and vegetables will help you stay healthy and motivated. I am no nutritionist, but have read my share of books and informational pieces regarding health and fitness. Keep the sugar to a minimum as well as the caffeine. With your own business, there is no time for the 3:00 slump. Stay hydrated and energized in natural ways, with nuts, berries and lots of water. Did you know a teaspoon of honey has the same effects as an energy drink? Try it!

Make sure to get at least 30 to 60 minutes of exercise each day. Find things that you enjoy doing. Play with your kids, walk around the block or take a bike ride. Exercise does not have to be painful. "No pain no gain" is the motto if your goal is to be a super model or a body builder, but for us normal women, it becomes the goal to simply move more and eat less!

The next key to persevering through the process is your relationships. Keep these in balance by making time for those important people in your life. Make date night a priority if you are married or dating, ensure there is time to play games with the kids and don't forget breakfast with your best friend at least once a month. And as my mom reminds me to make sure you listen to the Lord as He may bring a different best friend in your life at different times. His plan, remember? All work and no play do not a balanced woman make.

For those of us that are married, it is essential we not forget about our husbands and their needs. Yes, we both work, and hopefully you can find ways to share the household errands and chores, but continue to keep your man a priority over yourself and your business. He will be your biggest cheerleader when he knows he is still #1.

Finally, we can't neglect our rest. It is so important, as women, that we allow ourselves to rest. The Bible says 6 days' work, one day rest. We are wired for multi-tasking and at times feel guilty when we are not producing. If we own our own businesses, have families, friends and obligations, there has to be a day of rest. Allow yourself to rest one day a week, with no emails, phone calls or thinking of your business.

This allows you to recharge for the next week. Make sure your family knows you are taking that day of rest. They are not allowed to ask things of you on this day that are out of the ordinary. Sure, you will feed your family and make sure they are taken care of, but other than basic necessities, your day of rest should be a known thing. Communicate and remind those around you that if you are not able to recharge at some point you will burn out. This effect is far more negative in the long run than a simple day of rest that they allow you to have once a week.

The Women of Faith produced a study guide called Living a Life of Balance. It is an amazing resource if you want to dig deeper on the importance of balance. You can find it at your local bookstore or on the Women of Faith website.

Chapter 7 Questions to Ponder:

1. What is your reaction when the going gets tough?

2. Do you have a network of peers you can draw from? If not, where can you find these important people?

3. How balanced are you in looking at the list on page 62? Which area do you need to improve upon?

CHAPTER 8 –
LISA: A CASE STUDY IN PERSEVERANCE

LISA - Lisa grew up in the small town of Bossier City, Louisiana and had dreams of making it big like most young women do. As a single young mother she moved from small town USA to "the Big D" Dallas, Texas. She found that moving to a new city with zero contacts, financial or emotional support proved to be one of the biggest challenges to face.

She reluctantly took a support role for a top producer in the mortgage field in order to get a paycheck coming in, and start making contacts in the mortgage world in Dallas. It was humbling to go from being the top producer in Bossier to working for one in Dallas but just like her journey, she always tried to find ways to grow from the experience. After working her way up to being a top producer again in the mortgage field, over the next three years, she finally felt ready to venture out into the world of business partnership with her boyfriend and co-worker.

Opening a business with someone you are dating proved to be a big mistake for her. Every decision from business card logos to financial decisions became an emotional battle of wills between the couple. Control was the ugly monster they battled and the third party partner suffered being a part of all of it. Needless to say, after one year of the chaos, all parties decided that changes had to be made even though they had begun to make a profit during the first year in business. All three parties split and opened up independent companies who would be competitors down the road.

As soon as she stepped out to open her own corporation her daughter decided that she hated Dallas and wanted to go live with her father in Bossier City. It was an excruciatingly painful time of self-discovery for her- but it opened up the opportunity to dive head first into her new business. Somehow her most important priority – GOD got moved off of HIS throne in her life and the pursuit of money sat righteously upon the throne for a season. Lisa was still consistently serving, tithing and attending church but the business somehow had taken over every one of her waking moments, thoughts and emotions. Everything took a backseat and she was making more money that she had ever made in her life, or even thought she could have accomplished (400,000.00 per year). She bought the house on the golf course, the car, the shoes, the purses, the clothes, the front row hockey seats etc. Her business had expanded with locations in Texas, California and Louisiana. She had arrived but at what cost! One quiet morning while having quiet time, studying the word of God, she felt convicted by a scripture that talked about placing more value in your house than in God's house. Her heart felt so heavy and it began a season of introspection about who, and what, was taking priority in her life. This also began a season of illness that would eventually take almost everything she valued in life. The level of stress that comes with a life out of balance can do maximum damage. Lisa experienced multiple hospitalizations and surgeries which eventually caused a massive hemorrhage in finances. Two new locations which were not producing and her inability to produce herself caused a quick downfall of her house of cards. She had looming home foreclosure, car repossession, bankruptcy and eventually homelessness as a result.

Rising from the illness, then working as a valet and bartender brought about some major humbleness that was needed. She was reminded of what God's word says about building your life on the wrong foundation.

> *"If any man builds on this foundation using gold, silver, costly stones, wood, hay or straw, his work will be shown for what it is, because the Day will bring it to light. It will be revealed with fire, and the fire will test the quality of each man's work."*
> - (1 Cor 3:12-13 NIV)

Today she is back, self- employed, successful and with a business partner who complements her areas of weakness. Balance is so much more a part of her life and God is on HIS throne in her life. Here is what Lisa had to say when we sat down:

M: *What factors encouraged you to start your own business the first time?*

L: While I was working at a mortgage company, making money for others, a few partners and I decided to start our own business, so we would be able to make our own decisions, and keep the bulk of the money we made, instead of lining others' pockets.

M: *What were some of the obstacles you had to overcome?*

L: I was in a personal relationship with one of my business partners at the time.

Personalities and emotions played a big factor in our obstacles and not allowing others to use their strengths. We all wanted control.

M: *What is a key ingredient to a successful business?*

L: Putting God first in your business and decision making. Having humility and patience, and especially compromise are key ingredients.

M: *After the dissolution of the first business, why would you try again?*

L: The first mortgage business did not work because of the partners and personalities involved. I branched out on my own the second time and was very successful.

M: *Do fears ever creep in and cause you to think you have made a mistake?*

   What do you do when that happens?

L: Absolutely! I have to pray, pray, pray… and I have to believe that God has me where he wants me. I have to take those fearful thoughts captive and smack them like a fly!

M: *Do you consider yourself a successful business owner?*

L: Yes. I built my current business, which is actually the fourth business entity, and we have doubled our profits in one year.

M: *What advice would you give other women who want to move forward and start their new business?*

L: Putting God first is key. Be sure about the partners you go into business with. Make sure you can get along but have different strengths and weaknesses so you complement each other. Make sure they have a proven track record.

Have some money saved! This is a big one.

Make sure you have a support team around you, whether it is other business owners, friends, family, and mentors and so on.

And market, market, market!!

Lisa is Managing Partner for iTalent Consulting, Accounting & Finance in Dallas, Texas. They recruit talent for high level financial and accounting positions.

CHAPTER 9 –
7 KEY COMPONENTS TO EFFECTIVE TIME MANAGEMENT

It takes a certain personality type to start their own business, to have the self-confidence, support and trust in God to make it happen…it also takes a woman who desires time and freedom from a corporate or other type of structured environment. We are the women who act on our God-given desires, and who make it happen. We are also the women who may enjoy the occasional day off or lunch on the patio with a friend. When owning your own business, you may find the urge, especially if things are not going quite as you had hoped, to sit back and relax a bit. It is times like these when it is critical for you to step up your game. Don't give in to the negative thoughts you may have about the current period in time. Use this time to find new opportunities to network, volunteer, research, etc.

Throughout this chapter, we will explore seven key components to managing your time effectively and avoiding procrastination.

Whether you work from home or you have an office, your routine is important. Your morning routine is especially important. This sets the tone for the entire day. If you can take time to meditate, pray or reflect on scripture first thing in the morning, it will put you in the right mindset for the day. Be thankful and give praise for those things in your life…your ability to run your business, your health, your family. Enter the day with thanksgiving!

If at all possible, you will want to start your day off with some exercise. Morning exercise has been proven to burn more calories during the day, and it gets your blood flowing for energy during the day. Even just a 30 minute walk will make a difference. It is also crucial that you eat a healthy breakfast to keep the mental juices flowing.

If you work from your home, it is key to have a separate work space from your living space. Not only is it good for your mindset, it is a requirement to take the home office tax deduction, but that is a different discussion altogether, and I am not a tax advisor!

It is important to start work at the same time each day and dress for the day. Many people can work in their pajamas, but it is proven that if you feel good about yourself, you will be more productive. Occasionally, sure, wear your jammies till noon, but make these times a treat to yourself, not a daily occurrence.

By utilizing a separate workspace during working hours, this will allow you to focus on your business priorities, instead of getting off track with household duties, chores or children issues. It is also a key in feeling like you can disconnect from work once you quit for the day. Make sure to keep a healthy balance when it comes to working after hours. It is not recommended, but as a business owner, at times I will check my email after hours to see if there are any needs. This is acceptable, but keep it to a minimum or you will cause issues with your friends and family. Remember, a big reason for owning your own business is for freedom and time – time for yourself and your family, outside of the ties of another's' corporation or business.

Organization can be a big key in your time management process. If you do not have a current plan for keeping track of what you need to do, take these tips into account. I am a list maker. I live off of lists and my calendars. I love to make lists at the beginning of the week for all the crucial items I need to accomplish that week. In addition, each day, I will make a list for those things that should be done for that day.

If I do not get everything done for that day, I will add the leftover items to the next day's list. I either make my list at the end of the day for the next day, or first thing in the morning. List making can assist those who tend to be procrastinators. If you tend to put off those difficult tasks, write them down. Give them a priority and a due date. This will encourage you as the day approaches to make sure to get them done. Calendars are great in helping with this. Outlook calendars can keep track of to-do's as well as any appointments and tasks you have.

An organized workspace is equally as important. Act on every matter that comes your way. Prioritize the urgency of the matter or delegate it, but make sure to act on it regardless. This keeps procrastination at bay. There is an old saying about letting the paper pass your desk only once.

If you are the "old-school" type, planners work best. Jot down your ideas in your planner, and put your tasks and to-do's on a specific day so you can view these on a daily basis. If you continue to look at the task at hand, written in your planner, chances are you will complete it. The old adage, "out of sight, out of mind" is so true! For those of you who prefer technology, an electronic calendar on your smart phone, tablet, or simply using task manager within Outlook, works well.

And speaking of technology, this can be a great tool for your business, but it can also be a huge time-waster. Surfing the net can be a great resource but make sure to keep it within the parameters of being beneficial to your business. Many social networking sites can take us in directions that, before we know it, we have wasted hours at a time with nothing to show for it.

The best feeling for me is to be able to cross something off of my list or my planner. The accomplishment gives me energy to do something else. I know you may be different, but if you struggle with getting all the necessary things done each day, try a new method, like list making.

Delegation can be a big key for your time management success. Do not be afraid to delegate to other employees those tasks you do not need to directly be involved in. This is a test of a true leader. Someone who can lead by example and teach those around her has learned one of the most important skills in running a business. Delegation is your friend!

Lastly, a crucial key to time management is to make time during your day for yourself. For example, make yourself get up from the desk and take a few breaks each day. Take time to eat lunch away from the desk, or to take an afternoon walk. Making time in your schedule for you will keep you healthy and motivated, rather than burnt out and drained. You might even have to pencil these times into your calendar, if you are the "work-a-holic" type. But it is crucial to keeping good health and balance to make time for yourself throughout each day.

To sum up what you just read, the seven components we discussed in making the best use of your time are:

1. Daily Routine

2. Separate Work Space

3. Organization – Lists/Planners

4. Organized Workspace

5. Keep Technology Work Related and limit the time spent

6. Delegation

7. Make Time for Yourself

Chapter 9 Questions to Ponder:

1. Do you feel you are a good manager of your time? Why or Why Not?

2. What are the areas of your routine or organizational process that could use improvement?

3. How do you stay organized? If you have not thought about this before, now is the time to make sure you have the best way lined out for you to manage priorities.

CHAPTER 10 – NEW BUSINESS DEVELOPMENT

Developing new business tends to come easier for some than others. And it tends to have multiple meanings. In my business, dealing with clients and supplier partners means we have to continue to develop our business in many areas and in many ways.

We discussed lead generation in prior chapters so you will want to continue to find new and innovative ways to generate leads. The leads will turn into new business and to develop that business takes effort. Depending on your business model, this will mean different things. But in all businesses, communication is the key to development. If you bring on a new client, but soon move on to the next client, at some point the first client will feel neglected. To keep the business moving to the next level, communication via email, phone call, newsletters, helpful articles and in person meetings will keep your relationships fresh. I am a huge fan of the hand written note. For many reasons, I will send a note, whether it be a thank you for a recent meeting, or just a "thinking of you" and offering to assist in some way note.

Realtors do a great job of this by staying in constant contact. Postcards are great to send to clients as a thank you, reminder, or for asking for referrals. Referrals can be the best way to develop new business. If you have a satisfied customer, asking for their letter of recommendation can be a big boost for your business. Put their testimonial on LinkedIn, your website or on a reference list.

By asking your current satisfied clients for names of those they think you could assist, or sell to, is also a great way to develop new business. Don't be afraid to ask this question. If you have developed a great business relationship with your client, they will be more than happy to give you a name or two.

Keep your clients and customers in a tickler type file with information that will be helpful in the future. If you are an artist or sell jewelry, and you know the types of pieces that your clients are buying, keep them abreast when you have something new to showcase. Staying in front of your buyer is extremely important. When you have something interesting or valuable to share most people are receptive to the communication.

As I previously mentioned, I am a big fan of the handwritten note. There is power in a personalized thank you note, or other hand written card. Think outside of boring postcards and other marketing ideas, and send a handwritten card to one client, or prospective client a day. Be specific with your intentions. Let them know you appreciate their business and want them to be a customer for life! I recently sent some cards to people I had known for years, but had not been doing business with them. I had a great response.

Newsletters are always a great tool to use to stay in front of your clients. By incorporating helpful articles, educational information and industry events, the newsletter will more likely be read. Stay away from fillers like horoscopes, recipes and trivia unless those are related to your business. Pictures are always an attention getter as well. People love seeing pictures, especially of themselves. If you have an event, make sure to take pictures of your attendees or clients and incorporate that into your newsletter or publication. Your clients will look forward to getting your mail.

Think outside of the box when it comes to selling to your existing client base. Are there other areas you can assist them? Can you provide educational information that will position you as an industry expert? If they come to rely on you as the expert in your field, you will have a customer for life. The trust factor comes into play here as well. If your customer trusts you they will continue to buy from you.

Chapter 10 Questions to Ponder:

1. How are you currently developing new business?

2. Think about creative ways you can get in front of people to get more exposure for your field or business. You want to be known as an industry expert!

3. What is your referral plan? You need one! Even if it is simply to ask your current customers for one name.

CHAPTER 11 –
SOCIAL MEDIA

There are multiple books on how to fully utilize social media. The purpose of this chapter is to simply give you an overview of what is out there, how to incorporate the mediums into your business model and let you know it is not as scary as it may sound. The jury is still out as to whether it really helps your business grow, but it will depend on the type of business you have. It is also probably worth noting that by the time you read this, there will be countless new social media outlets that I don't even know about yet!

Facebook – Facebook is probably the most popular social media avenue right now. Most everyone is on Facebook, or has been on at one point or another, whether young or old. Make sure to keep your personal Facebook pages separate from your business Facebook pages, or keep a close watch on your personal page. If you don't separate them, you will not want to post those crazy bachelorette party pictures for all your clients to see. It won't create the most professional image, unless you have a party planning business. Or if you do post those types of pictures, make sure you do not "friend" your clients and associates on Facebook. Keep your Facebook personal page your close friends and family, and keep a business page for business associates.

Facebook has Pages that are free to create. You can upload your company logo and pictures, elaborate on what your business does, and invite people to "Like" your page for maximum exposure. Anytime you update your page, all the people who have liked your page will receive the updates. This is a great way to advertise any specials or sales you might be having. It is also a great place to post informational articles to continue the process of educating your audience. This will continue to help build trust with your existing clients and keep you in front of those future clients. Make sure to keep your Facebook pages updated and current or it will be a turn-off to those who visit.

I have "Liked" multiple pages such as my hairdresser and my travel agent. They post fun things like new hair styles, products that are beneficial as well as travel deals and great places to visit.

Facebook also has areas for advertisement if you have a marketing budget. We will talk more about this in Chapter 12. www.facebook.com

LinkedIn – This is the more professional of the social media sites where you can practically sell yourself and what you do online. LinkedIn is an online resume of sorts that allows you to showcase your experience and your accomplishments. It also allows you to connect with others in your industry because of who you are connected to. By "linking in" you build a huge online audience for posting and communicating.

LinkedIn is a great place to look for new prospects, clients and peers. There are multiple search features available, and when searching by industry, you are able to connect with people you may not normally even know of. We have come a long way from searching the yellow pages for leads. Now we have photos and resumes, contact information and more, at our fingertips.

LinkedIn groups are a great way to connect with others. There are multiple groups for every industry and business. There are even social groups that will tie you into others with the same type of interests. The message board forums allow for group discussions where you will again want to portray yourself as an industry expert. The higher your visibility the more chances for success.

As your business grows, LinkedIn also offers a great place to find employees and post job openings. You can search for great candidates yourself by using the search features and keywords. Recruiting Professionals, in every business, utilize LinkedIn because of the ease of use and instant exposure to all types of potential employees and candidates there are.

Make sure that once you join LinkedIn, you put a page together for your business, even if it is just your logo and a description of what your business does. This is a great way for people to find you on LinkedIn, and for your business to appear more professional and visible.

Make sure after you create your business page, you edit your own personal profile and choose this place of employment for your business. If you simply type in the name of your business but don't select the business you created, it will not show up when someone clicks on your business name on your own personal page.

The News section provides articles of all kinds to stay abreast of what is going on in the business world and in your industry. It is also a great place to find an article to share with your LinkedIn community, post on your Blog or share on your Facebook page to stay in front of your audience. www.linkedin.com

Twitter, Blogs and YouTube are other forms of social media that can keep you in front of your audience. You will want to research all forms of social media to find what works for your business.

Twitter, for my business, is the least effective way, but depending on your profession, it could be the most effective. Twitter is known for capturing one's events all day every day…this can be too much for some people and could get old quickly. You run the risk of losing your following if it is too much or irrelevant. However, if you are a celebrity it could work quite well! If you keep it business professional your tweeting could be an effective marketing tool.

The nice thing about Twitter is you can link it to your other Social Media accounts and by tweeting once, you will hit multiple other accounts simultaneously. www.twitter.com

You Tube is an effective tool by using video instead of words. This is a great way to display a "How to…" and get your name out there. As we discussed earlier, by being an expert in your field, you become a valuable resource to your clients. If you are comfortable in front of the camera, consider putting a short 2-3 minute video together that would highlight the best features of your business. You can do this with your own personal computer, if it has a camera, or use a simple video camera and upload the file to your computer for sharing. www.youtube.com

Post on your outlets regularly and keep the content up to date. Comment on others' posts and blogs to create community discussions and visibility. You want to become an expert in your field and be noticed.

There are also a few warnings regarding social media. Be careful about the time that you spend as you can get sidetracked and lose your focus. I have been known to be searching through profiles on LinkedIn only to find myself an hour later reading an article about a new store opening!

The avenues that social media can take you is part of its draw. It is meant to take you on a journey from person to person and interest to interest. So make sure not to end up wasting your valuable time by searching for non-relevant people or things.

Don't forget about the icons you can add to your website, or your auto signature on your email, to remind people to follow you on your social media sites. These are easy to grab and add to your sites. If you are unsure about how to do this, there are Help screens on each site to answer how to do this, plus multiple other answers to your social media questions.

Chapter 11 Questions to Ponder:

1. Do you feel social media can enhance your business?

2. If you are already utilizing social media think about ways you could improve on what you are currently doing. Are you updating your pages and posts regularly?

3. Brainstorm about creative ways to get your business name out in the social media world and which avenue would work best for your particular business model.

4. Who do you know that can help you with social media sites?

Draw from friends and acquaintances to get ideas and helpful hints on putting your social sites together. Start thinking outside of the box on ideas for your social media sites. Have fun and be creative!

CHAPTER 12 – MARKETING AND ADVERTISING

Marketing and branding your business is extremely important, however, do not make the mistake of spending a fortune right off the bat. You will want to ensure your branding encompasses what your business stands for. In addition, you will want to make sure you have all necessary pieces to complement each other.

When starting with your business name, make sure to brainstorm on what the meaning of your business is. There is a lot in a name. It took us forever to come up with our name. We searched the Internet for multiple meanings of what we wanted to convey with the name of our business. We bounced ideas off of other people constantly. But in the end, we agreed on initials of the partners names. This made us happy with the name and conveyed a message of quality that we wished to convey.

Moving on to your logo is the next daunting task. Search images of your name; find something that is appealing to you. Logos can be images, letters or simply your business name as long as you are consistent. Make sure coloring is easy on the eyes and the images or letters are easily recognizable. If you are not very artistic, there are multiple websites out there today that will practically put the logo together for you. Once the logo is put together, you pay a small fee for the rights to use it and the high resolution images that you will need for business cards.

Another great tool for logo design is a crowd sourcing website that will have the web community design a logo for you. Multiple logos will be designed and once you find one you like, you can bid on what you are willing to pay for it. This is a great way to get a professional logo at a lower cost.

When putting your marketing packages together, do not hesitate to seek out a professional. You want to make a good impression on your business cards, brochures and promotional material. It is better to do without in the beginning than present less than professional looking materials. In addition, as we move to the digital age, being "green" and all, consider electronic promotional materials, as opposed to paper. This will be much less expensive in the long run, and you will be surprised how many people don't really want your brochures after they have looked at them.

When we began our business, we felt like business cards were extremely important. We threw something together after long deliberations about our company name, and in the end, I wished we would have waited a little bit longer in creating our logo and business cards. We have changed our logo since the initial printing which caused us an additional expense. Had we just taken a little more time and not been so anxious, we would have saved ourselves some money. Even though we bought business cards twice, the initial purchase was extremely affordable. I would recommend, in the beginning, using an inexpensive printing service. There are multiple sites you can locate by searching the Internet that will print your cards for less than $10, or in some cases for free. The reason I recommend this in the beginning is most likely you will be anxious in getting started like we were. If you go this route, use an inexpensive card. Most likely you will change or update your logo, or even modify colors, etc., and you will save yourself some money in the beginning. You can even print them yourselves on your personal printer.

Once the cards are done, you will feel like you are truly in business! You will want to move on to how you will market yourself. Will you do print advertising, web advertising, brochures, one page slicks, etc.?

These are questions you will have to answer prior to getting started on your marketing pieces. Again, if you are not very artistic, you will want to consult a professional in getting at least one or two marketing pieces in hand.

If you are somewhat creative, Microsoft Publisher and other tools are available to create brochures, newsletters and ad slicks. With a few clicks, your verbiage and some pictures, you will be able to create your own pieces within a very short time.

Take your time with your marketing plan, and make sure you do exactly that, have a plan. Have a plan for getting your materials together, what they will be used for and how you will market yourself and get your name out there. I could have spent more time in this area. I feel like we created some things too quickly and we were not really sure where we would utilize each piece.

We now have a name and logo we all love, with an internal and external meaning. We have a basic marketing slick that can be sent to prospects that tells our story. We have updated our website twice to improve upon the quality. Make sure you have a call to action on everything you do marketing-wise. This would be a phone number to contact for more information, how to order your products or sign up for your services.

We chose not to pay for advertising due to the industry we are in. We did not feel our target market would act from print advertising, or even web advertising. These are areas you will want to research to see if it makes sense in your line of business. Many times you can end up in print advertising just by making yourself known. We will talk more about this in the Networking chapter, but articles and event photos are great to submit to publications that pertain to your business.

Blogging and utilizing social media outlets will keep you in front of your audience without paying for ad space. These outlets will also help by search engine optimization. This means how your business is found on the Internet. The more your name is out in cyberspace, the more well-known you become, and the more times you are likely to show up in the beginning pages of an Internet search.

A website is key for exposure to your business. Even if it is just a small website with just a few pages to give you a web presence and credibility. There are many tools available now and websites are inexpensive enough that everyone should have one.

If you are somewhat tech-savvy, you can put it together yourself, as all websites have templates to start with. If you still think a mouse is a small rodent, you will want to get help putting your site together. And even if you are somewhat tech savvy, be cautioned, as there are a lot of moving parts to designing a web page. Don't be scared, just cautious.

You will want to include in your website the key points of what you do, how you do it and some credible information about your company and yourself. Many times your website will be used just to validate your business.

Keep in mind, advertising can be very expensive, but at times it is worth it. Just make sure to do your homework and have a plan before you decide to execute. In the beginning, your dollars might be few, so you have to really utilize them in the way that will provide the highest rate of return.

Chapter 12 Questions to Ponder:

1. Have you decided on your image and branding (i.e. Logo)? What is the meaning behind it? Make sure to create something that is meaningful to you and will be memorable to others.

2. For your website, sit down and map out the content. What will the headings be? What will each heading contain?

3. Think about some creative ways you can advertise for little money. Drop off flyers at local businesses, at your church or local trade associations.

CHAPTER 13 – STACY: A CASE STUDY IN INDEPENDENCE

STACY - Stacy's story is similar to mine in that she had many years of property management experience prior to taking the plunge. After being a successful executive, she knew there was a gap in the industry in her niche of revenue management.

Stacy was a single woman who made this decision on her own, without support of a husband. To me, this is such an inspiration, as a support team is so important during this time. During this interview you will learn the people who were there for her for support as well as Stacy's definition of success.

> M: *What were some of the initial challenges you experienced in starting your business on your own?*
>
> S: Definitely fear and uncertainty. I am a planner so to take this leap without

knowing for sure how it would turn out was huge for me. Not only that, but I was surprised by the number of naysayers I encountered when sharing my desire to start my own business.

M: *Talk about some of the support you had around you. Who was your "cheerleader" in the beginning?*

S: I was in a relationship with someone and he was really the driving force behind my decision. Without him I truly do not think I would have made this decision on my own. Now, being out of that relationship, I realize I do have the confidence and the drive to do it on my own. I think I needed him at that time to spur me on. I also have two very best friends that I have known since High School who have been behind me all the way. They keep me grounded by giving me the worst case scenario to think about when I am letting fear and doubt take over. After I realize the worst case is not the end of the world I keep moving.

M: *Have you ever second guessed your decision?*

S: Only once or twice a day! All the time! When things get stressful or difficult I question if I have done the right thing. But I always come back to the freedom and flexibility I have with my own business. I also like to keep in mind my ten year plan and where I want to be in the future. This keeps me moving in the right direction.

M: *Are you at the level of success you thought you would be at this point in your journey?*

S: I actually anticipated faster growth but by growing slower than expected we were able to work out some kinks. I feel there are definite advantages to growing at a slower pace and I am at peace with where we are as a company today.

M: *What is the most difficult thing about having your own business?*

S: There is no safety net of relying on the larger organization for things like insurance, IT support, etc. I think there are things we take for granted when working for established organizations. Not having these support systems at my fingertips took some getting used to, but the advantage is that I learned a lot of new things along the way.

M: *What is the best thing?*

S: Definitely the flexibility.

M: *If doing it all over, would you do everything the same way?*

S: I lost some valuable time in the beginning because shortly after I started the business, my personal relationship ended. I started the business somewhat dependent on the support of my significant other and I wasn't sure if I could, or even wanted to, continue on my own. After taking ample time to do some serious soul searching I decided to move forward with my decision. In hindsight I wish I would have come out of the gate faster and not dwelled on my personal situation as much.

M: *At what point do you consider yourself successful?*

S: My goal, is to live life, travel and build a company that is employee based and provides a good working environment for others. I want to have a company that is well known in the industry and has a good reputation. I do not see success as a specific dollar amount. I see success as having employees that feel valued and clients who feel like they truly have a partner who is working to help them meet their goals and objectives.

Stacy's company, Revenue Edge, is a successful Revenue Management firm based in Dallas, TX. She currently services property management companies across the United States.

CHAPTER 14 - NETWORKING

Networking is an important and effective part of growing your business. When I first began, I knew there were people I wanted to get in front of and learn from. I had made a few different contacts on Social Media and I started researching the women who owned their own businesses. I sought them out because I knew I could learn from them...what to do and most importantly, what not to do.

You will be surprised, when you begin to reach out, how willing others are to share information and advice with you. If you are lucky enough to seek out and meet with others in your specific industry, even better.

There are many networking opportunities these days, but keep in mind, many groups are geared toward a social networking atmosphere. Many groups are going by the title of networking group when they are in fact partying or dating groups. If your goal is to grow your business, you will want to make sure you find the groups and the people that will help you reach your goals. In turn, you will want to make sure you can add something to their lives as well.

After seeking out a few women who owned their own businesses successfully, I realized there were more and more than I ever thought around me. I decided to start my own group. I found a venue that would accommodate 5-10 women comfortably, and scheduled a meeting once a month. Coffee shops are great for these types of meetings as it is a casual and fun environment. I would prepare some various topics of discussion and participants would leave some topics that they would like to discuss more in the future. We currently have 15 members that meet periodically and it is a blessing to be able to share ideas, encourage and motivate one another.

Not only did I find meeting with them one on one was beneficial, but our regular meetings became an important part of my life and very beneficial to my business. We have certain stresses as business owners and especially as women. We have to continue to balance our lives as we run and grow our companies. It is so nice to have a group of like-minded women around me to bounce ideas off of, get advice from or simply vent from a stressful event.

Volunteering is a great way to network. This is also a great way to help stay balanced as we talked about in Chapter 4. In our business there are multiple associations. I have joined multiple committees within these associations, participated in trade shows, golf tournaments and various other activities to stay engaged. These networking avenues will pay huge dividends for your business because relationships are really what businesses are built on. When you are volunteering, you are building relationships with others and working together for a common goal. Seek out associations and organizations within your industry and join a committee or volunteer to do something. Find what you are passionate about and donate some time to this cause. Not only will you reap huge business benefits, you are doing something for someone else, and that makes the world a better place.

We talked about LinkedIn previously in the Social Media chapter, but now we are going into more detail about how the groups can help you with your networking endeavors. When you search for groups on LinkedIn, make sure you use keywords from your industry or type of business. You will find more than you imagined when you start searching. Join the groups that are interesting to you or that are in your field of expertise. Not only will you be able to participate in forums within these groups, you will be connected to more people on LinkedIn due to being in the same groups. This opens up the doors for more communication between you and your potential clients. You have the ability to connect because you belong to the same groups. Posting and commenting are a great way to get visibility, just make sure you are posting and commenting in a professional manner. If you are selling something, make sure to keep your posts and comments "unsalesy". By this I mean, you are the expert in your field. Use your knowledge and expertise in a way that helps the others in the group, gets your name out there, but does not come across as you are only trying to sell them something. Give them something that shows them what is in it for them.

When you have the opportunity to network by holding a lunch gathering, it is a great way to meet people and generate new business. The lunch & learn concept is a way to get a small group of people together, preferably prospective clients, and educate them about something you are the expert on. The idea is to invite some of those on your Dream List like we discussed in Chapter 3, or previous clients who you want to get back in front of. Provide a nice breakfast or lunch, provide them some valuable information (this is the key because people are extremely busy) and at the end provide a call to action.

If you are providing an educational forum, tie it in to how they could benefit from being your client in the future. You will want to give them an opportunity to sign up for your services, purchase your products or partner with you to gain long-term benefits. People love a free lunch, so this tends to be a popular way to gain exposure. It might cost a little bit, but if you gain clients, it can be worth it. There are also ways you may be able to have the food sponsored depending on your business. Many restaurants today also provide a nice banquet or meeting room at no cost as long as you purchase the food there.

Networking is all about building relationships and getting in front of people. One of the most important key factors to remember about networking is to look for those opportunities to work with those you already know. For example, if you are shopping for car insurance, think about your current networking group, the people at your church or your Facebook friends. Who sells insurance? If you support those around you when you are looking for something, others will do the same with you.

If you are the shy type, Social Media is a great place for you to start. If you like being in front of others, the lunch & learn will pay off. Team players should plug in and volunteer within their local charities and associations. If you can incorporate all of these networking ideas into your business plan you will have multiple opportunities to meet others and share ideas, gain clients and help others in the process.

Chapter 14 Questions to Ponder:

1. Do you currently know of networking opportunities? If not, have you thought about starting your own?

2. What kinds of volunteer opportunities are in your community? This is where real bonding and sharing can take place. Great relationships can be built through volunteering together.

3. What are you an expert in that you can hold a lunch and learn, or partner with someone to do this? Or how about write an article if you prefer that media outlet instead? Submit to your local newspaper or trade publication to be published.

CHAPTER 15 – REBECCA: A CASE STUDY FROM TRAGEDY TO TRIUMPH

REBECCA – We pick up Rebecca's story with her role as a financial planner. She was on a path of climbing the corporate ladder and on a pursuit of money and her 'then definition' of success. Her plan was radically changed after she had a car accident that put her in the hospital and out of work for two years with mounting medical bills.

While the accident was not her fault, the other party was underinsured. For this reason Rebecca began a passionate interest in learning about the insurance business. After seeing a Dr. in Spain that was finally able to diagnose her correctly, she was on the path to recovery, but realized there had to be something more for her life than the 80+ hour weeks in the financial planning business.

When I talked with Rebecca, she tells us what really helped her get to the level she is at today.

M: *What was the deciding factor in your decision to start your own business?*

R: My son Braden. While recovering for over 30 days, confined to lying flat on my back, I had a lot of time to contemplate my life. I realized I wanted more time with my son than what my career was allowing.

M: *Talk about some of the support you had around you. Who was your "cheerleader" in the beginning?*

R: My family is scattered all over the world, from Spain to Norway, so I really didn't have any one close here. My girlfriends from my church were really my support system.

M: *Have you ever second guessed your decision?*

R: Oh yes. Every day. I replay those tapes in my head that remind me of the comforts I am leaving behind with my day job.

M: *Are you at the level of success you thought you would be at this point in your journey?*

R: Depends on how you define success. I am totally happy with where I am with my business today. I feel like I can breathe again…whereas before I was smothered by all the self-imposed goals and responsibilities.

M: *What is the most difficult thing about having your own business?*

R: The uncertainty of the next prospect or wondering where the money will come from.

M: *What is the best thing?*

R: Time with my family and the flexibility to do what I need and want to do.

M: *If doing it all over, would you do everything the same way?*

R: I think so. I don't think it would have as much meaning without the process I had to go through. I don't think I would have as much passion for my industry had things gone differently.

M: *At what point do you consider yourself successful?*

R: Right now I feel it. My definition of success

is worlds apart now than what it was years ago. I can pick up my son from school and take him to get a snow cone which is worth more than any money or title.

Rebecca is Owner and Agent at Farmers Insurance Group in Little Elm, Texas. Her focus and passion is educating and informing people about how important having the proper insurance is. She lives with her son Braden in Little Elm, TX.

CHAPTER 16 –
INSPIRING OTHERS

So this is the chapter that really got me to thinking about writing this book. As I did my research after the start of the business, and I began meeting with other women who had already gone before me, I realized they were coming away energized. When I was the one asking most of the questions and trying to find my way, they were being encouraged and inspired as well.

I had an "a-ha" moment after a phone call with a woman who had owned her own business for almost ten years and we talked for over an hour. I was trying to pick her brain and gather nuggets of information that would help me get started, encourage me and hopefully share information about possible clients. She began to ask me questions that seemed rather basic to me. She said she was not very good at certain things and asked my opinion of how to gain new business. I thought to myself, how can she, at ten years of being successful, be asking me how to gain new business? But my answers impressed even me. I didn't really know where it was coming from. I started to realize that I had more knowledge than I gave myself credit for. I realized that even though some people are successful, they still do not know everything. That is when I thought there is a huge need for us as women, to help and inspire each other. We have to utilize our own gifts and talents and share those talents and gifts with others. We have to help each other where we fall short so we can all be successful. It was that moment I said, I am going to start writing.

It is amazing to me how certain things flow together and just intertwine. For example, businesses are going to be successful because people enjoy you and want to be around you. People want to do business with people they like. That is a proven fact.

How do you impact the world around you? Do you truly care about the people you come in contact with? If not, you really aren't living out your purpose under God's plan. Do you even know your purpose? Our purpose is not that difficult to figure out. In Rick Warren's book "The Purpose Driven Life" he says we are on this earth for God's pleasure and to use our gifts and talents to make the world a better place. If you are starting your own business, you know what your gifts and talents are. Your gifts and talents are what give you that spring in your step. They are what motivate you to get out of bed in the morning. Most likely, it is whatever you are doing with your business because you have passion about it.

Take it to the next level and make sure you are sharing your gifts with the world. We were not created to simply exist. We were created to give God pleasure as well as impact other human beings. Luke 10:27 says "Love The Lord Your God with all your heart and love your neighbor as yourself." There are actually multiple references in the Bible that instruct us to love our neighbors as ourselves.

Interact with others and really take the time to know them. When you take the time to listen to others and honestly care about them, no matter who they are, you will know what it means to "live".

General Colin Powell said in a speech while I was at a conference in Orlando, "…treat everyone with dignity and respect, as they matter…because they do." By showing that kind of respect to each and every person, you will inspire others to do their job better, to be a better person and to simply look at life a little differently. Every human being matters. They were put on this earth just as you and I, with a purpose and a plan. Let's treat them as such. When you give respect to the people who clean up the offices at night, you are an inspiration. When you understand the valet employees are trying to earn a living to put themselves through college to have a better life, you are an inspiration. Take the time and SEE people. This will make you an inspiration to others and you will, in turn, gain a perspective like no other.

Chapter 16 Questions to Ponder:

1. Do you feel you inspire others today?

2. What types of activities do you currently do, where you interact with other women, that you could make a concerted effort to encourage others?

3. How can you make the world a better place during the course of your workday?

CHAPTER 17 –
MELODY: A CASE STUDY IN INSPIRATION

MELODY – Melody's story takes her from a child in a foreign country, the youngest sister of 5 siblings, working her way from schoolgirl to successful American business woman.

Melody was always very competitive with her siblings and this drove her to excel in school and beyond. In 1974, after high school, she followed her brother to the United States to go to college for Engineering. After a while at school, and being homesick, she made the trip back home and this is when she met her husband. They became engaged, but Melody wanted to go back to the States and finish school.

After about six long months without her fiancé, she had not completed her schooling but she decided it was time to go back home. This is when she and her husband got married and started a family. Melody knew the opportunities were much greater in the U.S.

and when her children were about 5 and 7, they decided to make the permanent move to America for a new beginning.

Because she never finished school she went to work where the opportunities were. At this point in her life, it was an ice cream shop. As with school and everything else Melody did, she excelled in her job and was promoted quickly. She took great pride in every job, even as an ice cream scooper.

From there she went to retail sales and quickly moved up the chain in those companies as well. Melody was the perfect example of determination.

Because her dream was to finish school, Melody decided to pursue her schooling career and go back. She ended up with a degree in Nursing as she always had a passion for children and helping people.

After graduation, she landed a job as a nurse technician and again rose through the ranks as head nurse. Part of her determination comes from wanting to help people and part of it comes from being a people pleaser. She is the kind of person who won't say no, so she ends up being the "go-to" person to get things done. She is someone others count on.

After observing a family member with their business, and learning from them, she made a complete change from the nursing field and started her own moving company. In 2000 Ameritex Movers was born.

Due to her tenacity and passion for succeeding in all that she does, the change of direction had no bearing on Melody's success.

I had the opportunity to sit down and ask Melody a few key questions about her career and her success. Here is what she had to say:

M: *After 13 years in business, how do you stay competitive in the moving business?*

Melody: I set myself apart from all the others. I feel customer service is extremely important and I don't believe in having answering services or messages. I ensure a live person answers our phones at all times. I think referrals are a crucial part of our success and if our clients are not happy they will not refer.

M: *Moving is so different than nursing. Do you miss the nursing field?*

Melody: A little. I still do some nursing and caretaking on the side for special needs children. This allows me to give back to the community and do what I always loved to do. I believe what goes around comes around, and I am passionate about serving others.

M: *What is the best part of owning your own business?*

Melody: The flexibility. I am at a point where the money is good now and I am able to be flexible with my time.

M: *Do you consider yourself successful?*

Melody: Yes. I try to be humble and live a simple life, but I am a hard worker. I work hard for the life we have today. I have inspired my daughter to also start her moving business in Houston and she has as many trucks as we do in Dallas!

M: *Is your husband involved in your business?*

Melody: Yes. He is involved in the business somewhat with our trucks, as well as our building needs. We just recently decided to expand our office space and he is working on the renovation of this space. He is my soul mate.

Melody is the Owner of Ameritex Movers in Dallas, TX. She has been married to the love of her life for 38 years and hopes to continue to work and assist the D/FW community with moves. She feels this is how she stays youthful and energetic…keep working!

CHAPTER 18 - MEASURING SUCCESS

How do we measure our success?

This is critical for you to understand BEFORE you go too far. Today's society will say a certain dollar amount is success. I do not necessarily agree with that philosophy. Certainly, you are in business to make money, but that should not be your primary focus. Consider what it usually means to have money. Typically, that entails more debt. The more we make, the more we spend. It is proven that money does not make you happy.

In a survey in February 2013 by bankrate.com, they found a higher percentage of Americans have more credit card debt than they have in savings. In fact, according to another poll, 80% of Americans have debt of some kind. While we see it as a necessary evil on one hand, for our homes and sometimes automobiles, it is proven that it can get out of hand.

What does this do to us as human beings? We

tend to worry more, about how we will pay our bills on time, or we even become discontent with what we do have by continuously looking for the next bigger, better, shinier thing.

In the beginning stages of my business, I will admit, I had the same school of thought. I knew I wanted freedom and time, as mentioned in an earlier chapter, but early on I did not really grasp the depth of what that meant. I was like most business people in that I was always working toward the next big title or to achieve financial gains. Spending insurmountable hours, neglecting family members, friends and health, just to attain the next level is a common occurrence in America.

God has shown me, by trusting Him for our needs, He will provide in so many ways. Psalm 37 is a blueprint for the promise that He has made to us.

PSALM 37:3-9 SAYS:

TRUST IN THE LORD AND DO GOOD;
DWELL IN THE LAND AND ENJOY SAFE PASTURE.
TAKE DELIGHT IN THE LORD,
AND HE WILL GIVE YOU THE DESIRES OF YOUR HEART.

COMMIT YOUR WAY TO THE LORD;
TRUST IN HIM AND HE WILL DO THIS:
HE WILL MAKE YOUR RIGHTEOUS REWARD SHINE LIKE

THE DAWN,
YOUR VINDICATION LIKE THE NOONDAY SUN.

BE STILL BEFORE THE LORD
AND WAIT PATIENTLY FOR HIM;
DO NOT FRET WHEN PEOPLE SUCCEED IN THEIR WAYS,
WHEN THEY CARRY OUT THEIR WICKED SCHEMES.

REFRAIN FROM ANGER AND TURN FROM WRATH;
DO NOT FRET—IT LEADS ONLY TO EVIL.
FOR THOSE WHO ARE EVIL WILL BE DESTROYED,
BUT THOSE WHO HOPE IN THE LORD WILL INHERIT THE
LAND. (PS 37:3-9 NIV)

Only you can decide how you will measure your success, but I can tell you from my experiences, as well as talking with many others, the best measurement of success is trusting God with your business and all aspects of your life. It is not always easy and sometimes I forget who I am relying on, but I quickly come back around to trusting Him when I decide to let go of the control. God is in control anyway, so when we take the reins from Him we are only doing ourselves a disservice. Give it a try and document the peace you have while not worrying and allowing Him to provide for you, in His way.

My business and my life have reached a true success point. Is that because my net worth is six or seven figures? Absolutely not. In fact, we are still in the building stages of our business, and there are no guarantees that we will ever see seven figures. We have the potential and the resources to get there, but I am still eager to see what God is going to do with The MaRK Advantage. Does He want it to be our sole business, or is there something out there that we still do not know about? We are still unsure; but we keep the options open; so if God chooses to move me in another direction I will be willing.

Since inception, we have yet to touch our savings. Each quarter our profits are rising and our expenses continue to stay slim, under 10% is ideal. The measuring stick for me today is this:

- I get to work with my best friend and life partner every day

- I have a home office so I do not have to fight traffic at rush hour

- I have the ability to choose who I will and will not do business with

- I have been home after school for my boys, and as teens, this might not seem so important, but studies have shown, this is an even more critical time to be home for your children. This is when their self-esteem blossoms or hibernates, and when left alone there are too many opportunities for getting into the wrong things.

- I have the time to exercise regularly with my husband and plan and cook healthy meals together

- My husband has been off of blood pressure medicine since coming to work with me due to less stress

- I have more opportunities to give back to the community with my flexible schedule

- When my work is done in fewer hours, I do not have to look for busy work to get in my eight hours to please a boss

- I can go to a matinee movie on my lunch break if I want to

- Shall I keep going

suc•cess /sək'ses/

Noun - The accomplishment of an aim or purpose.2.

What is your "aim or purpose"?

I don't see success as throwing money around or filling up a ten car garage. On the contrary; I think that "stuff" continues to keep us in bondage. Release it, and the thought of your next purchase, and enjoy **_THIS_** day you have been given right here and now. And then, you will know you are successful!

Chapter 18 Questions to Ponder:

1. How do you measure success?

2. Do you measure success the same way today as you did a few years ago?

3. What are the top 3 things you would have when you consider yourself successful?

Similar to the case studies throughout this book, there are many women who have taken this step toward independence and freedom from the corporate world.

Check out these comments from other women who have taken the plunge and started their own businesses, as well as the encouragement they shared with each other…they had fears and thoughts just as you probably do. We all need a little push and who better to give it than other women…

Starting Over and Loving It!

Janelle says on a public forum site:

After years as a call center director/ manager, I decided to take the plunge in 2010 and open my own business in a completely different field - home health care. It's been hard, frustrating, scary and challenging! BUT, it has also been the best decision I've ever made. So many people I know are struggling with similar job problems, however, we all have some amazing strengths that can roll over to new areas (like customer care/ sales/business dev.) which can be stepping stones for new opportunities.

Just wondering — are others doing similar things??

Katie R • Yes! I lost my corporate job (of 8 years) in January of 2011, and it was the biggest blessing. I now own my own Wardrobe Consulting and Personal Shopping business and I absolutely love it. It definitely hasn't always been easy, but I am doing what I love and that is one of the most important things to me.

Ana G • Yes Janelle, I too have taken the plunge and have decided to go after a dream I have had for a couple of years. As a seasoned HR professional I decided to use my experience and talents and put them to good use within my own community here in Jacksonville. My journey will take me on a different route and my goal is to flourish my non-profit. The Hispanic Institute for Life and Leadership (The H.I.L.L.) of Northeast FL will focus on becoming a premier professional development institute and job placement referral agency for skilled and professional Latinos. We have a huge need for these services here in the greater

Jacksonville area and I hope to be able to make an impact. As a new business owner don't forget to seriously consider how you could service Latino customers in this community. Our buying power is over a billion dollars currently in our area alone. My hope is to be able to find you those Spanish Speaking employees when you need them. Good luck on your venture!

Laura P • I am! 10 months ago I started my business but it's a very related field to my 20 years of experience. It has been the hardest thing I've ever done. I agree, best decision as well! It requires Moxi and in most cases some cash to invest. Thank you for sharing!

Lindsey S • I have a very similar story to all of yours. But I knew that things would come back together after the 2008 fall out. I put it out in the universe that I wanted to "write checks to people to great things in the world" In 2011 A great friend of mine and wonderful ski partner gave me the opportunity to launch a new software company that focuses on small "local" businesses. With my background I have been able to help hundreds of small business expand their sales. The State of Colorado SBDC saw what I was doing and just recently asked me to join their team part time! It is going to be a busy winter... I start my new job with the state of Colorado this week! Wish me luck :)

Katherine H • I just am starting my 30th year in running owning birthing changing my own business!!!!So proud of you ... Keep this going no matter what.

Angelina M • Janelle - congrats on your switch into such a wonderful field. I'm actually looking for callers that can help my company instead of me hiring a call center so if you ever want to explore doing some freelance call work let me know. Or if you know of some people that might want to I would be interested.

Janelle H • Thanks for all of the comments and sharing your stories. It's sometimes nice to know that I'm not the only one out there that had to recreate myself! I was laid off of 3 call centers in 10 years when they were outsourced overseas, but I can't complain because I really learned a lot with each of the companies. My pharma/insurance customer care and sales centers were my favorite and I think that was what drove me to turn to healthcare.

Ana • as a transplant from Tucson, AZ, I love what you are doing to help the Hispanic community! I just hired our first Spanish speaking CNA last week and I know she will be a big plus to our business. With our patent list growing, it's wonderful to be able to assist others. Best of luck everyone!

Kaya G • Really wanting to, but my biggest fear is income.... It's an idea I've developed based on my experience, yet it is such a big launch, and I wish I would have some help and finance. I do have an opportunity for financial backing, but I have yet pulled my strategic business plan, it's in my head.

Creig D • Kaya, you just mentioned your first step. Business plan. Why are you holding back? Fear keeps a lot of people from doing what they love. Take it one step at a time. Don't wait until you're 60, and regret having not tried. Fear sometimes can push you into each step that you have to make. The journey is wonderful and the destination you reach is very rewarding! :) Don't miss the boat! You already have more than most........a financial backer!!! Fantastic!!!

Olga M • Thanks Janelle for getting this started. It is good to see we are not alone in our fears, great to see that so many women are starting their business and succeeding. I am a graphic designer and opened up my studio last year.

Noelle I • @Kaya - you can do this!!! You just need to keep honing your business plan and make sure you have support before you pull the trigger. If you feel that you need the security, you can start your business while you are working a more corporate gig. Many go that route! You will be great!

Lara R • Citi actually gave me the opportunity to reinvent myself with my move from Human Resources (where I'd worked for 10 years in total) over to the Marketing Team doing social media. I'd always regretted never getting a chance to put my degree focusing on marketing/international business to use it the work setting. I appreciated their supporting me on such a change and it's been a wonderful experience for me. It hasn't been without challenges along the way, but it was great to see it wasn't too late to make a change!

Erin L • So great to hear everyone's stories! I too am making a transition from corporate compensation analyst to jewelry designer... I wouldn't have left my corporate job for what a lot of people consider a 'hobby', but I really left the corporate job because I wanted to stay at home with my baby. I knew I would want to stay at home for at least the 1st year, so we planned financially to be able to get by on my husband's salary and we saved my entire corporate salary for almost a year & half before baby was born.

Now that she is 1 year old, I want to work again, but I want something flexible where I can control my hours... so here I am making jewelry whenever i can ~
My advice to anyone making the switch~ budget and save before you quit the corporate job... and believe in yourself :)

Works Cited

<u>Love and Respect</u> - Emerson Eggerichs - Integrity Publishers - 2004 - Hardback

<u>Worth Every Penny</u> - Sarah Petty, Erin Verbeck - Greenleaf Book Group - 2012 - Hardback

<u>The Proper Care and Feeding of Husbands</u> - September 2006 - By Laura Schlesinger - HarperCollins - 2006.09.26 - Paperback

<u>The Purpose Driven Life</u> - Rick Warren - Running Press Book Publishers - 2003 – Hardback

<u>The Ultimate Sales Machine</u> - Chet Holmes - Portfolio - 2008 - Paperback

<u>Living a Life of Balance, Women of Faith Bible Studies</u> – Foreword by Marilyn Meburg - THOMAS NELSON - 2005 - PAPERBACK

Acknowledgements:

I am first and foremost thankful to God for giving me the vision and the fortitude to write this book. Without Him I am nothing.

I am truly thankful to the ladies whose stories have inspired me, and changed my life.

To Lisa, one of my best friends, thank you for always being here for me through the good and the bad.

To Stacy, thank you for your inspiration. Before I even knew you I was inspired. You are such a strong woman.

To Melody, thank you for sharing your background and story with me. It is truly amazing and such a story of strength and perseverance.

Rebecca, thank you for the leap out on your own into a business that you have so much passion for to truly make a difference in others' lives as well as to be the best mother you can be.

Angela, thank you for being so transparent to share your journey to transform the lives and the health of people you come in contact with.

There are many other stories of women out there, but these ladies took the time to share with me in hopes of making a difference for someone else.

Thank you to my family and friends who constantly encouraged, edited and read multiple versions, gave feedback and advice. Special thanks to my mom, dad and Susan for their loving guidance and support.

Thank you to Melissa (Mel) Lawson with Melzone Productions, Multimedia Graphic Design, for her amazing work on this cover!

And finally, thank you to my amazing husband, who stood by me as I wrote this book, shared our lives with strangers, and never once told me I could not do it. You are my rock and my life.

More about the Author:

Melissa Palmer has a 20+ year history in Property Management and has held various positions at both the site and corporate levels. In her experience she has assisted over 60 property management companies totaling over 350,000 units. Melissa is a Certified Apartment Manager (CAM) through the National Apartment Association and attended The University of North Texas in Denton, Texas. She lives in McKinney, Texas with her husband, and business partner, Keith, and together they have 5 boys.

Melissa and Keith are both very involved in their church and also donate their time and efforts to the Samaritan Inn, a local homeless program that helps provide a brighter future for those less fortunate.

The MaRK Advantage is a thriving boutique consulting business with clients across the country, from Texas to Idaho. Their mission is to serve each client as if it were their only one, giving them superior service and attention.

The MaRK Advantage partners with companies to streamline and standardize their purchasing practices to increase profits and efficiencies.

Never stop dreaming!

www.ingramcontent.com/pod-product-compliance
Lightning Source LLC
Chambersburg PA
CBHW030753180526
45163CB00003B/1010